P9-DNN-120

BEYOND
2012

Photo © Anna Digate

About the Author

James Endredy is a teacher, mentor, and guide to thousands of people through his books and workshops. After a series of life tragedies and mystical experiences as a teenager, he changed direction from his Catholic upbringing and embarked on a lifelong spiritual journey to encounter the mysteries of life and death and why we are all here. For over twenty-five years, he has learned shamanic practices from all over the globe while also studying with kawiteros, lamas, siddhas, roadmen, and leaders in the modern fields of ecopsychology, bioregionalism, and sustainable living. James also worked for ten years with Mexican shamanic researcher Victor Sanchez, learning to share shamanic practices with modern people.

James was given the name of Ulu Temai, or Ulu Temay (the spelling varies throughout the Wirrarika), which translates to "new ray of the sun" or "new arrow of the sun." This name was an honor bestowed on him by the eldest shaman in James's Wirrarika community in recognition of his dedication to the shamanic path.

On a daily level, his experiences have inspired him to live a sustainable lifestyle as much as possible while still working within mainstream society. He writes, leads workshops, mentors private clients, visits schools and community centers, speaks at bookstores, and volunteers in his community. His books, including *Ecoshamanism* (Llewellyn, 2005), have thus far been published in four languages. James leads ceremonies and workshops related to the teachings of the First Shamans and the material in his books. For more information, visit his website at www. jamesendredy.com.

BEYOND 2012

JAMES ENDREDY

A Shaman's Call to Personal Change and the
Transformation of Global Consciousness

Llewellyn Publications
Woodbury, Minnesota

Beyond 2012: A Shaman's Call to Personal Change and the Transformation of Global Consciousness © 2008 by James Endredy. All rights reserved. No part of this book may be used or reproduced in any manner whatsoever, including Internet usage, without written permission from Llewellyn Publications, except in the case of brief quotations embodied in critical articles and reviews.

FIRST EDITION
Second Printing, 2008

Book design by Rebecca Zins
Cover design by Kevin R. Brown
Background leaf image by Brand X Pictures
Edgar Cayce photo used by permission of the Edgar Cayce Foundation

Library of Congress Cataloging-in-Publication Data
Endredy, James.
  Beyond 2012 : a Shaman's call to personal change and the
transformation of global consciousness / James Endredy.—1st ed.
      p. cm.
  Includes bibliographical references and index.
   ISBN 978-0-7387-1158-4
  1. Prophecies (Occultism) 2. Civilization, Modern. 3.
Mayas—Prophecies. 4. Change (Psychology) 5. Shamanism. I. Title.
   BF1809.E53 2008
   203´.2—dc22
                      2007042314

Llewellyn Worldwide does not participate in, endorse, or have any authority or responsibility concerning private business transactions between our authors and the public.

All mail addressed to the author is forwarded but the publisher cannot, unless specifically instructed by the author, give out an address or phone number.

Any Internet references contained in this work are current at publication time, but the publisher cannot guarantee that a specific location will continue to be maintained. Please refer to the publisher's website for links to authors' websites and other sources.

Llewellyn Publications
A Division of Llewellyn Worldwide, Ltd.
2143 Wooddale Drive, Dept. 978-0-7387-1158-4
Woodbury, MN 55125-2989
www.llewellyn.com

Printed in the United States of America
on 15% post-consumer waste recycled paper

Other Books by James Endredy

Ecoshamanism:
Sacred Practices of Unity, Power & Earth Healing
(Llewellyn, 2005)

Earthwalks for Body and Spirit:
Exercises to Restore Our Sacred Bond with the Earth
(Bear & Company, 2002)

The Journey of Tunuri and the Blue Deer:
A Huichol Indian Story
(Bear Cub Books, 2003)
INTERNATIONAL READING ASSOCIATION 2004 NOTABLE LIST
AMERICAS AWARD 2003 FINALIST

Contents

PART TWO:
The First Shamans Speak

PART THREE:
Practical Applications of the First Shamans' Teachings

Introduction

I never planned to write this book. That is to say, only a few years ago, the topic of 2012 was just beginning to rise significantly in the consciousness of people throughout the world, and the importance of this time period was still somewhat obscure. But now we can see interest in the implications of the 2012 time period all around us. International magazines, such as *Time* and *National Geographic*, as well as major television channels, such as the History Channel and Discovery Channel, are running feature stories and full-length programs having to do with 2012, the End of Days, catastrophic Earth changes, Armageddon, the Mayan calendar, and many other topics revolving around the great time of transformation we are living in: the period leading up to 2012.

It was a series of opportunities and synchronistic events that led me to write what you are now reading—to put my energy toward sharing a positive approach in these times of change. For that is the encouraging information that I have received from both the First Shamans and my own research. Human consciousness is key to what will actually happen in 2012 and the years leading up to it. The positive message in this is that we are, for the most part, in control of our destiny. But we need to change. By all indications, the human enterprise is out of control on this planet. The good news is that we humans are adaptable, and I believe that with wiser use of our technologies, more compassion between people, and greater education and understanding of the interconnection of all life, we are up for the challenges that lay ahead for us.

This book began with an invitation from Llewellyn to do another project with them after my *Ecoshamanism* book of 2005. Consequently, I was invited to participate in the 2006 INATS convention in Denver, and it was there that I had the fortune to spend time with some of the key people at Llewellyn, such as publisher Bill Krause and publicity manager Alison Aten. Even though publishing books is certainly a business, after spending just a few days with the Llewellyn managers and sales staff, I knew for sure that they truly love what they do and are intentionally engaged in making a positive difference in this world.

Upon returning home from the convention, I communicated with acquisitions editor Lisa Finander about various book ideas, and she tossed up the idea about a book on 2012 from a shamanic perspective. I liked the idea, but to be honest, at that time I had a few other more important books on my mind that I felt needed to come out.

The next afternoon, I taught my class at the Institute for Ecotourism and afterward joined some friends for a drink at the resort there. Well, wouldn't you know that a friend brought for me the April 3rd edition of *Time* magazine, which was all about how global warming is detrimentally affecting the biosphere, and one article revealed how James Hansen, NASA's chief climate scientist, was accusing the Bush administration of muzzling him when reporting on the dramatic effects of global warming and censoring him when his opinions differed with the president's.

Now, for those of you familiar with my work, you know that this news was not very shocking to me. I have been trying to help elevate ecological awareness and reconnect people with the natural world for many years through my books and workshops. And I never trusted this president, since the last election was rigged. But what did affect me in a profound way was that here we finally had an international magazine from the United States that was actually reporting the truth about these issues. With a circulation of over 4 million, this was truly great news.

On my way home that night, I stopped at my mailbox and found that another friend had sent me a very interesting DVD by Ian Xel Lungold about 2012 and the Mayan calendar. The DVD evoked memories for me of the 1980s and '90s, when I had spent many years exploring the Mayan ruins and temples and living for periods of time with the modern Maya people. But I was also getting the distinct feeling that I was being guided toward something special and to keep open to all possibilities. It seemed more than coincidental that directly after Llewellyn suggested I write a book about 2012, the *Time* magazine articles literally were placed in my lap the same day I received a DVD about 2012 and the Mayan calendar…

The clincher came a few days later. I was waiting for a friend in a coffee shop and decided to check out the reading material they had on a rack. The first book I touched was *Maya Cosmogenesis 2012* by John Major Jenkins. There were also two more books about 2012 on that small rack. Since it was Sedona, Arizona, one of the New Age capitals of the world, it wasn't surprising to find these kinds of books in a coffee shop, but adding up the synchronicities of the past few days, it was becoming clear that something really big was coming.

I went home and searched the Internet for information about 2012. What I found was very troubling. Much of the information was about the Mayan calendar ending on December 21, 2012, and the implications of that, but most of the rest was all about doomsday and the end of the world! It was in that moment I decided that Llewellyn's suggestion for a book on 2012 was not only appropriate but necessary.

For the next few weeks, I admittedly floundered as to how I was going to tackle the subject. I read some books and searched some more on the Internet. Some of what I found was very interesting, but mostly it was downright depressing. So much of it was doom and gloom, and much of the rest was off-the-chart New Age wishful thinking, like how we will all "ascend" spiritually and leave this world behind in 2012.

I knew then that I needed to receive my guidance from sources outside the purely human sphere, so I went to speak with Grandfather Fire, something I had been doing for many years since learning the technique from the Wirrarika Indian shamans. What specifically happened next I will save for the opening chapter, but suffice it to say that I received the guidance I needed, and even more than that I received actual material for this book. The importance and timeliness of this material cannot be overstated, and once I began to receive it I knew I had to make this project my first priority. I spoke with the First Shamans many times and put together a sample for Llewellyn, which they immediately contracted to be this book.

In the end, I would have to say that not only had I not previously planned to write this book, on many levels I didn't really even write it at all. I truly feel, in an even stronger way than with my previous books, that this material came through me from the First Shamans as a direct response to the many crises we face leading into the next decade, and because a positive attitude, coupled with real solutions inspired by heightened states of awareness, understanding, and compassion, is where human consciousness is now heading.

I truly hope this book will hold your attention, light up some brain cells, and inspire you to join in the movement of conscious co-creation as we evolve into more mature human beings. The time has passed for the building of arks or the digging of shelters so we might escape destruction. It's time now for us to transform into wise stewards of our planet and employ positive strategies for the renewed health of our home planet and all its species, including our fellow human beings.

I believe we can do it. Do you?

JAMES ENDREDY
New Year's Day, 2007
Sedona, AZ

PART ONE:
Living in a Time of Transformation

Grandfather Fire sharing with me his light, warmth, and numinous wisdom. (Photo: Nancy Bartell)

SEEKING HELP FROM THE FIRST SHAMANS

"Greetings and welcome, Abuelo Fuego Tataiwari," I say with great respect as the first flames of the sacred fire spark into life in front of me. "Thank you for being with me once again, for enlightening the shadows, for your heat, your flowing energy, your wisdom, and your protection in the night. I offer you the food that sustains you—the fuel for your body and my energy for your mind—for I have a special request of you this night."

Yes, Jim, I know of your request. I have been waiting for you to wake up enough to hear this message. I have given it to you before, but you weren't ready to hear it. I am glad that you have progressed this far in the teachings that you hear when I call.

"So you will help me with this, Abuelo?"

Of course I will help you. But you know there will have to be offerings. Reciprocation. As always, I will expect you to be true to your offerings.

"What would you have of me, Abuelo?"

In order for you to receive the full depth of what I'm to share with you, you must first work more on your energy. Be even clearer, and empty your vessel. First, I want you to stop putting so much energy into thinking of this new lady in your life.

"I've been working on that, but it's hard!"

This is my time to talk, hijo,[1] *can I expect you to keep interrupting?*

"No, Abuelo,[2] I'm listening."

This situation with the new love you have found will unfold naturally; there is no need for you to give up so much of your energy to it. Release your attempts to control it. It will do you no good. Be true; that is all that is expected of you. If you are true, then there's nothing to worry about. Do you understand?

"Yes, Abuelo, I understand."

Good. Now, your garden. You have been lazy. The energy of Grandmother Growth will be needed as we spend more time together in the following weeks. Balance yourself. Spend time with your Grandmother, take better care of the beings that provide your energy. Plant more seeds so the miracle of creation and growth is infused into your being.

And one more thing.

"Yes, Abuelo."

Before you come to me next, I want you to fast for three days and then make a deep sweat in the lodge. I want your energy to be clear and strong so that you will be able to feel all the colors of my light so that you may spread it in the proper way when you write for your people.

Go now, and return when you have prepared yourself properly.

"Thank you, Abuelo."

||||||||||||||||||||||||||||||||||||||||||||||||||||||

And so it goes in front of Grandfather Fire. The only thing you can be is real. The only thing you can offer is your energy in helping to spread the light. There is no asking without offering. That is what makes this relationship so special and so balanced.

All of us feel the luminous energy in the flowing flames of the fire. Ever since I can remember, the fire has attracted me and mesmerized my mind. But it wasn't until I began living and learning from people that enjoy a happy and peaceful subsistence lifestyle without roads, electricity, and artificial light that I began to comprehend much more about the fire—especially when the fire is brought forth with intention, connection, and the desire for numinous wisdom.

---

1   *hijo* = son

2   *abuelo* = grandfather, *fuego* = fire

That is what the teachers who set me on this path, the Wirrarika shamans, have shared with me—and what I hope to share with you.

|||||||||||||||||||||||||||||||||||||||||||||||||||||||||||||||||||

Now you might be asking—is it really possible to receive wisdom from the fire? To actually have a conversation? Could it be true that the flowing energy of the fire can impart divine knowledge? These were questions that I wrestled with for many years when I started participating in ceremonies with the Wirrarika and got to see firsthand how the shamans would "sing the voice" of Grandfather Fire, Tataiwari, and how all the people would go to the sacred fire and speak their truths, ask their questions, and send their prayers. At first, and for quite a long time, I didn't get it. I mean, I wanted to believe, and I was able to observe and respect this tradition firsthand and see its effects on the Wirrarika, but I couldn't claim to see, hear, or feel what they did.

Then I was invited to participate in a pilgrimage to the sacred peyote desert of Wirikuta, where the Wirrarika go to "find their lives" and communicate directly with the Kakaiyeri[3] by entering into their house. And it was there that my relationship with the fire changed forever. In one glorious night, after much fasting, little sleep, a lot of prayer, and surrounded by the luminous energy of that sacred desert and my human companions, I witnessed the fire rise up and merge with the stars. In that moment, I understood from a place completely separate from my rational mind that the energy of the fire right in front of me was the same as the energy I could see twinkling in the heavens above me. Then, as I continued to concentrate on this scene, I began to see the image of the messenger Kahullumari, the blue deer,[4] rising on the tips of the flames. It was Kahullumari who taught me to converse with Grandfather Fire.

Kahullumari instructed me to release myself completely to the flames. He told me that I was one and the same as the fire, so there was nothing to fear—that the spark of the fire lived in my heart (the electrical impulses that kept it beating) and in my brain (through the firing of my neural pathways). That the fire of our sun, Tayau (the son of Grandfather Fire), was the energy in all the food that nourished my body and kept

---

3 Kakaiyeri = Wirrarika name for deities and spirits of nature

4 Kahullumari is the blue deer spirit who is the guide, messenger, and guardian of the sacred Wirikuta desert. From the footprints of Kahullumari grow the *hikuri* (peyote) cactus. The blue deer emanates the light of the First Shaman, Grandfather Fire.

The fire and I are one. (These photos have not been re-
touched or altered in any way. Photos: Nancy Bartell)

me alive and warm. To connect with the fire, then, was simply to merge the fire of my human organism with the sacred fire in front of me. All that was necessary to do that was intention.

I will talk more about the intent that goes into bringing forth the sacred fire. But what happened that magical night was that my intent was strong and clear—I wanted more than anything to talk with the fire, to be a part of the Wirrarika ceremony in a way I never could before.

I will never forget what happened next, for I started to speak. But what I was saying wasn't coming from me: it was coming from the fire. The strangest thing was that I could hear myself speaking, but I had not a clue as to what I was saying. The speaking then turned into a sort of chant-song.[5]

After I'm not sure how long, the chanting stopped, and I looked up from the fire and across the flames to meet eyes with the shaman that was sitting across from me. In that moment, I finally got it. I saw the fire alive in the shaman's eyes. Then his whole body transformed into a luminous and flowing organism of light. He and the fire were the same. I and the fire were the same.

I looked around, and all my companions appeared as flowing light. I was surrounded by a circle of fires! Then the shaman (the largest of the flowing lights) began to "speak" to the flowing light next to him. This appeared to me as his light flowing and mixing with the one beside him. They "spoke" together for a time, and then the shaman turned and "spoke" to me.

What he basically said was, "Welcome."

Time had no meaning in those moments, so I have no idea how long it lasted, but when my perception of my companions was back to me seeing them as their physical bodies, the shaman again spoke to the man next to him (his assistant, for lack of a better word), who was a younger man and a good friend of mine. The old shaman did not speak Spanish well, and I spoke little Wirrarika, so my friend translated.

The shaman told me what I had been chanting through the fire. Grandfather Fire spoke about how I was to be an emissary between the Kakaiyeri and my people—about

---

5 I write about this in my book *Ecoshamanism*; a chant-song is a spontaneous, free-flowing, dynamic interaction between the individual and nature.

what my role was to be and what my task was. I was to share the knowledge of the Kakaiyeri with the people. As long as I did that and did not keep the knowledge to myself for simply empowering myself, I would continue to be taught and gain knowledge and wisdom.

The shaman asked if I would agree to the terms, and I accepted. In front of Grandfather Fire and my companions, I had to state that promise out loud, and I did.

I see your energy is much clearer and stronger this time, hijo. You have balanced your energetic relationship with Tricia?

"Yes, Abuelo, and I have spoken to her about it."

Very good. And what of your Grandmother?

"I've been tending my garden more mindfully; it is starting to look and feel better."

Is that all?

"What do you mean?"

I know you have spoken to her many times in the past. Why, then, don't you speak to her now, in your garden?

"I'm not sure. I mean, I feel her when I work the soil and tend my plants. I give thanks when I harvest from the garden. I even speak to her sometimes. But in my garden, I don't hear her speak back—not like I hear you."

You must pay attention to this, hijo. Your Grandmother is very wise and speaks only when it is important. I am the helper to what you call Shaman, those that can hear my voice clearly. I am a communicator. She is all about action, creation. To hear her voice, you must be completely open. But you can do it. In the past, you have heard her voice only in the sacred places where the veil is thinner. Now you must awaken to her in a new way. You must offer her something for her time, for she is very busy. I will let you work that out with her. That is your lesson for today. Go now, and return once you have spoken to her.

"Thank you, Abuelo."

The Wirrarika consider the First Shamans to be Grandmother Growth, Nakawé, and Grandfather Fire, Tataiwari. Tataiwari is like the patron saint to human shamans because he is a communicator. Shamans receive divine messages from him. But that does not make Nakawé less important; on the contrary. She is considered to be the First Shaman. She was here before all else. She provides the energy of life to the planet, and she also instructs the moon in keeping Mother Earth on its tilt so that Father Sun does not burn us with his power.

For women, due to the womb and their inherent creative energies, it is easier to converse with Nakawé. But even so, Nakawé tends to let Tataiwari do most of the talking with humans. She is always there, she is confident in her power, and she will speak up when she wants to make her point. At the time I am writing this chapter, I have conversed with her directly only a handful of times—but those times have been powerful, life-changing events for me.

When Tataiwari told me to awaken to her more fully, I instantly understood why, especially for the task I had been given in writing this book. The truth is, I had initially prepared the outline for this book from conversations only with Tataiwari. Boy, would that have been a mistake! I understand balance, but it didn't occur to me that Nakawé was a shaman who could speak to me the way Tataiwari does. I'm grateful that the First Shamans are so wise …

Shrine and altar offerings for Grandmother Growth. (Photo: Nancy Bartell, altar painting: Cher Lyn)

You have built me a shrine, hijo, how nice!

"Yes, Grandmother. I know that we have spoken a few times before, when I have entered the earth during ceremony[6] and in some of the sacred places. But my intention is to get to know you better, and I would like to invite you to join me with my work."

It is good that you have come to me. Your people have forgotten the face of their Mother and of their Grandmother. You will help them to remember, yes?

"I have received the message to do so, Grandmother. But there is so much I don't know, don't understand. I need guidance and knowledge. I know so little about what is truly happening. Sometimes I just want to cry or yell with frustration over what I see my people doing."

You are not alone in your work, hijo. Continue to act with care and respect toward your Mother. She is injured and crying. Help her and you help everyone. If you do that, I will be there for you. When your Grandfather speaks, he speaks for all the Kakaiyeri. And he knows my mind. But in certain moments, I will instruct you myself if you stay true to your path. You have much work to do; it's best that you start right away. I fear time is running short for your people. Transformation is needed and will come, whether they know it or not. The way this will happen will be decided by their actions. Listen to your Grandfather. Do the very best you can. That is all that is asked of you.

"Thank you, Abuela."

Our Mother is injured and crying. Transformation is needed. The outcome will be determined by our actions.

Strong words. What exactly do they mean? Of course, I have plenty ideas of my own, but what is the truth? Lots of people are talking about a transformation in consciousness that is happening right now. But what does that look like? Are we better off helping it or hindering it? How does this transformation relate to the earth changes we are also experiencing? How can we further help Mother Earth?

These are the questions that led me to ask Tataiwari for guidance, once I realized the answers, in some cases, were better off coming from a purely nonhuman sphere of thinking. But where do the answers from the First Shamans come from?

---

6   Information on the embrace of the earth ceremony can be found in *Ecoshamanism*.

chapter 1

When I connect with Grandfather Fire and Grandmother Growth, there is no doubt that in some moments there is a melding of my energy with theirs, my thoughts with theirs. This happens in a similar way to what happens when we talk with people. So one could say that when the First Shamans speak through me, there is certainly a part of me that comes through. For example, when they speak through me they use my words and my language. When they speak through the Wirrarika shamans, they use their words and their language.

But be sure that this is much more than my simply projecting my mind and thoughts to somehow imagine that the First Shamans are speaking through me. Most of what they tell me is completely new to me and unexpected. Many times I don't even know what I'm saying, so I either have a tape recorder running or someone else there to tell me what was said.

So how can this possibly happen? I will attempt to explain; there are two main components to this. The first is intent, and the second is experience. Neither one can do this alone. You can have all the intent in the world that you want to connect with the fire, but without the experience of interacting and learning little by little how to do it, you stand little chance. It is like someone who has never played baseball wanting to hit a ball thrown by a professional pitcher. It takes years of dedicated practice and thousands upon thousands of swings of the bat during countless games in order to acquire that skill.

The same goes for experience. You could be someone living outdoors your whole life, using fire for warmth and to cook your food many thousands of times, and never hear the voice of the fire speak to you.

So it is the combination of strong and clear intention coupled with the experience of thousands of fires brought to life in a sacred way, not simply for warmth or cooking but specifically for connecting, that allowed me to break the barrier of purely self-reflective thought and connect to these sources of divine energy.

After my first connection to the fire that was deep enough for him to speak through me, which I have briefly recounted previously here, it took me many more years to develop the skills used to share the wisdom I write about in this book. You see, on that first magical night I was being helped by people and forces that I didn't have in my everyday life. The Wirrarika people have such clear energy and such a deep connection to the First Shamans that just being with them helped raise my energy and shift my perception. The sacred peyote desert that was the setting for that magical night has an energy conducive to visions like I have never felt anywhere else. And the arduous trip to the desert, filled with periodic stops to sacred sites along the way, also contributed to enhance my psychic abilities that night.

You can imagine how frustrating it was to return from that trip and not be able to reproduce what had happened to me that night. I felt like I had done something wrong so that the fire did not want to speak to me again. And in a way, that was true. It is so easy to fall back into the hypnotized state of modern humanity (which is something I will get into more in upcoming chapters).

The thing that saved me was my continued devotion and desire to change my life. I spent years and hundreds upon hundreds of nights sitting with the sacred fire and speaking to him before I slowly began to hear his responses. As we will see, Grandfather Fire shares with us how consciousness and matter are but ripples in the same pond. All knowledge is thus interconnected, and touching the wisdom of the fire is about learning how to swim to other areas of the pond. This first started happening to me as I attempted to share the light of the sacred fire with work groups. Having groups of people come to the sacred fire and open their hearts slowly proved to the First Shamans that I was true to the path they had set me on. I began to hear the fire respond to the people I was working with. Gradually, group after group, I began to hear the fire speaking through me in order to help the people that had come to the fire with intention.

Although I would never compare myself to those old Wirrarika shamans that spend a lifetime with Tataiwari as a central figure in their lives, I know that through the sheer volume of intentional experiences I've had swimming with the fire to other areas of the pond, I now have a similar light behind my eyes as they do. I now see the fire behind my eyes even during the course of my everyday life, even while sitting in front of this computer. And that is why I can now connect as a conduit for the fire and share the wisdom that the First Shamans are requiring me to share ...

You have spoken to Grandmother, hijo?

"Yes, Grandfather, and she had some powerful things to say—many of which I don't truly understand."

It is good that you do not pretend to know the answers. We have much work to do in order for you to fully understand. Much of this work you must do without me, so that you can claim the knowledge yourself. That is the only way to truly learn.

"I'm not sure I understand, Grandfather. I thought that you would help me in delivering your message to the people."

Yes, hijo, but first you must realize for yourself where your people are and how they got there. That is your first assignment. Look to the cultures that have not forgotten the face of their Mother. Then look at your culture. In a deeper way than you have ever seen before, look what HAS happened and what is happening NOW. Your Grandmother has told you about the imminent transformation. But do not simply take her word for it. Thoroughly investigate this on your own. Look for signs, trends, omens. Open your heart and your mind. Use your intellect combined with your intuition. Once you have peered into the mind and heart of your people, we will speak more of the transformation, for then you will be better prepared for what I have to tell you.

And so it was that I started on this journey of knowledge. At first, it was inspired from a silent calling from Grandfather Fire, for he felt it was time for the people to hear his message. Next was awakening to Grandmother Growth. Now I was being asked to become a seeker of answers again, as I have been most of my life.

Chapter 2

2012 Prophecies and Science

Our species is facing perhaps the greatest test of its history.

We have the knowledge to be fully conscious human beings that live in synergy with our planet, but we also have the capacity and technology to create environmental devastation on a scale that could all but wipe us out. So which of these paths will we take, and what is ahead for us?

More and more people are now looking toward the year 2012 as the time when we will find out. On one hand, we have ancient prophecies that point to 2012 as the end of the world—or at least the end of the world as we know it. On the other hand, many of our top scientists around the globe are now saying that within four to five years (around 2012) we will have reached the "tipping point" with regard to human environmental impact on our planet. Once this tipping point is reached, there is no going back: the earth will no longer be able to provide adequately for all its inhabitants, and human suffering throughout the globe will reach epidemic and catastrophic proportions.

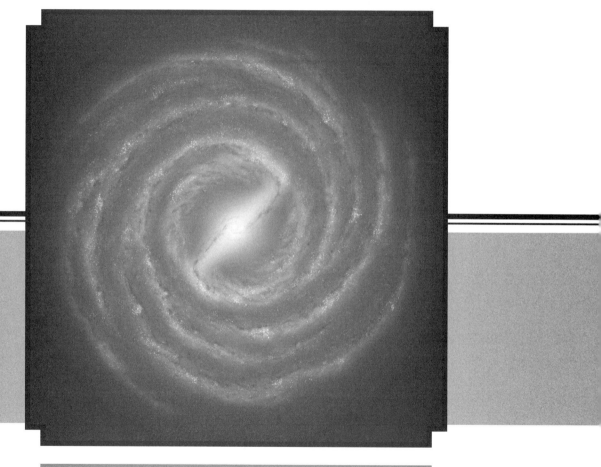

NASA illustration of the galactic core of our Milky Way galaxy. At the very center is a black hole 3 million times heavier than our sun. Its gravitational pull, so powerful that not even light can escape from its surface, affects the motion of dust, gas, and even stars throughout the region. Could our solar system's alignment with this center affect our lives, as many scientists now believe? (Photo © R. Hurt (SSC), JPL-Caltech, NASA)

If ancient apocalyptic prophecies come true via some type of natural disaster, there isn't much we can do to prevent the consequences. Meteorites, volcanoes, and earthquakes are still far beyond our control. But what *is* within our control is the way we live now and how prepared we can be if such a disaster should strike.

In looking at the science and probability of an uncontrollable natural planetary disaster in the near future, which I will explore later in this chapter, it seems very unlikely that this will be the case, at least not in the time frame around the year 2012.

The more likely scenario for the next decade therefore concentrates on human activity and the corresponding effects to our planet.

On the one path, we have a scenario where we break through our collective hypnosis of cultures based on never-ending economic growth. This happens as a critical mass of people recognize the necessity for change so that social and economic reforms come from the bulk of people that make up society. In this way, both business leaders and politicians recognize the demands and expectations of the people and respond with solutions that replace our current system of resource consumption (burning of fossil fuels, clear-cutting of forests, etc.) with systems based on infinite and recyclable resources (solar, wind, biotechnologies, etc).

The other path is the scenario of breakdown. Here we have the continuation of what we have right now: nations, ethnic groups, and religious fanatics continue to fight over finite resources and fanatical ideals. Instead of pursuing sustainable solutions, money and resources are continually diverted to increased military supremacy and acquisition of the remaining finite resources of the planet. At the same time, human environmental impact continues to increase, and as a result, weather patterns continue to change and the human population continues to increase so that food shortages, water pollution, and disease escalate to the point where human suffering reaches catastrophic proportions.

Some say that we have a choice as to what lies ahead in our future. Others stick to the view that we are living out a destiny that is beyond our control. So which is it? Let's look deeper into both scenarios.

2012 Prophecies

mayan cosmology

Overwhelmingly, the year 2012 has been planted into the human psyche as a year of both hope and fear by the many researchers of the Mayan calendar. Popular author John Major Jenkins has put forth the proposal that a rare alignment of our sun with the center of our galaxy was calculated by the Maya, and they chose that date in the future to end their calendar. By our Gregorian calendar, that date is 12/21/2012.

However, focusing on this date leads to many questions:

- How accurate are we able to correlate dates of the 260-day Mayan calendar with our Western Gregorian calendar?
- Do we know precisely *where* the center of our galaxy is and when our sun will align with it?
- When this alignment occurs, what, if anything, will happen to us or our planet?
- Whether or not the Mayan calendar ends on precisely 12/21/2012, why did the Maya have an end to their calendar at all? What is the meaning of this end?

Many researchers agree with the 12/21/2012 end date, but there are other prominent researchers who don't. Some Mayan scholars have reported a discrepancy in the calculations, making the true end date 12/23/2012, while well-known author Carl Johan Calleman calculates the date to be October 28, 2011. Other researchers point to dates in 2023.

There has been much debate recently as to the true end date of the Mayan calendar, but it seems clear that it will happen in the next decade or so. However, the implications of this are equally vague and open to interpretation. Jenkins has calculated the time period of 1998–2240 as the significant range of our sun's alignment to the galactic center and corresponds this important event not only to the Mayan end date but also to year 6000 of the Jewish calendar (the dawn of the seventh shemittah—AD 2240), Islamic cosmology, and the Hindu-Vedic chakra model. With 2021 being the period when our sun completes its crossing of the galactic equator, he views humanity's collective expectations toward 2012 as a trigger point for our creating a new world. In other words, we still have the power to create our own reality.

However, Calleman and others believe that the evidence clearly shows that we are on an evolutionary time schedule—that creation is continually speeding up. In his study of Mayan cosmology and its correlations to the various periods of evolution on our planet, he predicts that October 28, 2011, is when the very purpose of creation will be fulfilled: "It is when all things are brought together and all conflicting ways of being, acting, and thinking will be resolved and unified in a light that makes it possible for everyone to understand everyone else and everything at once."[7]

In my extensive time visiting ancient Mayan ruins and working with modern Mayan shamans, I have come to believe that the Mayan calendar ending on 2012 of our calendar doesn't signify the literal "end of the world" but rather *the end of the world as we know it*. Furthermore, the Mayan sacred calendar, the Tolkin, can be used as a tool of transformation during this time period; more on that in chapter 7.

hopi

Many Native American myths, legends, and prophecies tell of previous "worlds" that humanity has passed through. During each of these time periods, humanity evolved and grew until reaching great heights of achievement, but in each case they ultimately failed to walk in balance with Mother Earth and so were cleansed from the earth's body by the powers that rule the world: fire, water, wind, and soil. There are far too many prophecies and legends to cover even a small amount in this book; however, there is one tribe in particular whose prophecies and way of life stand out and therefore are being taken very seriously in these times of great change: the Hopi.

The Hopi are an extremely peaceful people that have endured countless trials and still maintain their independence from the "white man's" claim on their ancestral homeland, which is now located within the state of Arizona. Hopi mythology is complex, and as the tribe has endured more and more of its people being assimilated into modern culture, debate as to the correct interpretations of their legends is ongoing, even within the tribe. So the best I can do, and with no disrespect for my Hopi friends, is to boil down some of the well-agreed-on versions of their oral history and prophecies.

---

7   Carl Johan Calleman, *The Mayan Calendar and the Transformation of Consciousness* (Rochester, NY: Bear & Company, 2004), 215.

According to Hopi mythology, an infinite creative force referred to as Taiowa created the universe and brought forth an individual named Sotuknang, who was commanded to create lesser beings for our planet. Thus, the twins (a concept found in many ancient cultures of the Americas) Poquanghoya and Palongawhoya were brought forth and given the task of keeping Earth rotating properly, with one twin stationed at the North Pole and the other at the South Pole.

It is said that at the dawn of time (the First World), people were attuned with the universe, the Earth Mother, and the infinite (Spirit). But eventually the people began to lose this connection, and the doorway between the physical body and the spirit world began to close. Taiowa would not have this and so instructed Sotuknang to destroy the world and everyone in it except for those still attuned with Spirit. Those that were to be spared were led to the center of the world where the Ant People lived, and then all of the volcanoes of the world erupted and an all-consuming fire engulfed and destroyed the First World.

After the fires had subsided, the people came up from their shelter and entered the Second World. But again, the people lived until they forgot their connection to their origin with the Great Spirit, and so Sotuknang was ordered to destroy the world once again. The people to be spared again hid underground with the Ant People. This time, Poquanghoya and Palongawhoya were ordered to leave their posts at the poles and allow Earth to spin out of control. Earth flipped over and everything was destroyed by ice (the science behind this idea of a pole shift will be discussed later in this chapter). After the ice had melted enough for the people to return, they came up from their shelter and began the Third World.

The Third World was very corrupt, and this time the earth was purified by water. The chosen people this time were instructed to make sealed vessels, and when this was done Taiowa sent waves taller than mountains. Continents broke apart and sunk. Incredible rains fell. Then it all stopped, and when the vessels of the chosen people finally arrived at a new coastline, they emerged into the Fourth World, which is the world we are living in now.

The final stage of Hopi prophecy refers to the "great day of purification," which many believe will be soon in coming, as many signs leading to the end of the Fourth World have already come to pass: the white man would bring wagons hooked together but pulled by something other than a horse; railroads have fulfilled this prophecy. Then the white man would make roads in the sky, cobwebs in the air, and great lines across the land. Airline routes, vapor trails, and electric lines have fulfilled this prophecy.

Hopi prophecy also includes the invention of a "gourd full of ashes" that would burn the land, cause rivers to boil, spread an incurable disease, and prevent anything from growing in the soil for many years. The atomic bomb fulfilled this prophecy.

Finally, it is said that the white man would build his house in the sky, and this would mark the beginning of catastrophic earth changes. This would be the final sign that man has lost balance with nature and that widespread famine, plague, and wars were imminent. To many Hopi, the American space station Skylab is this "house in the sky."

It is important to know that when the Hopi elders were seeing the fulfillment of their prophecies leading toward the end of our Fourth World, they decided to make public their ancient prophecies. As early as 1948, they attempted to speak to the United Nations General Assembly. According to Hopi prophecy, the Hopi have been given the responsibility to care for the land of this continent and to share the message of the necessity for humans to be in balance with nature. This message was to be shared with the leaders of assembled nations from around the world in a great house made of mica that stands on the eastern shore of their land. The Hopi elders, in 1948, interpreted this to be the United Nations building.

Twice the Hopi elders were turned away when they asked to speak before the council. Finally, in 1976, at a United Nations-sponsored conference in British Columbia, they were allowed to speak their important message and to warn all people of the impending doom if we do not stop our destruction and desecration of the earth.

This is but a very concise portrayal of Hopi prophecy and their role in these times of great change. Similar to my Wirrarika mentors, the Hopi people believe that their ceremonies and rituals are helping to keep balance in the world, but if they are made to stop, the world will be destroyed once again. This, to me, is actually a message of hope, for in both the Wirrarika and Hopi cosmology there is one important factor: human consciousness. Both of these ancient tribes believe that we can awaken from the suicidal course we are now on, and that human consciousness will decide the ultimate outcome of the great day of purification.

The Last Judgment, painted by Michelangelo and his assistants for the
Sistine Chapel. (Image: Wikipedia.org)

christian prophecies

Since recent surveys show that our culture still has more people that consider themselves to be Christian than any other religious group, I will now summarize some important points in relation to Christian eschatology, which for our purposes here will be defined as the Christian study of its religious beliefs concerning all future and final events (End Times) as documented in the Bible.

Prophetic interpretation in Christian eschatology is a tricky subject, and it is not my intention to be biased one way or the other, but rather to present information that is relevant to this book and that you could explore further on your own, should you choose to do so.

Very concisely, there are four main perspectives to Christian eschatology:

- The HISTORICIST abides by scripture for the fulfillment of prophecies and the religious significance in past or present historical events.
- The PRETERIST abides by the book of Revelation and believes that most or all of the prophecies in that book have already been fulfilled.
- The FUTURIST looks for religious significance for the present time in events that are thought to be future in history or beyond history.
- The IDEALIST looks for regularities, patterns, or laws of history or of the internal life that are of perpetual religious significance. Additionally, some interpretations are purely metaphorical.

So the obstacle we have here, as is usually the case with the Bible, is interpretation. Because of that, I will simply lay down some significant passages and leave the interpreting to you.

In Isaiah's prophecy 13:13, we find a striking similarity to the end of the Hopi Second World, when the world was let loose and spun out of control: "Therefore I will shake the heavens, and the earth shall remove out of her place, in the wrath of the Lord of hosts, and in the day of his fierce anger."

In the New Testament, the central event that will rock the world will be the Second Coming of Christ. But before that happens, we hear from Matthew in 24:6–7 that signs of the end of the age include "wars and rumors of wars" and that "nation will rise against nation, kingdom against kingdom: and there shall be famines, and pestilences, and earthquakes, in [diverse] places." The final moments sound even darker: "Immediately after the tribulation of those days shall the sun be darkened, and the moon shall not give her light, and the stars shall fall from heaven, and the powers of the heavens shall be shaken" (24:29).

In 2 Peter 3:10, we also find a correlation to Hopi prophecy: destruction of the world by fire. "The heavens will disappear with a roar; the elements will be destroyed by fire, and the earth and everything in it will be laid bare."

There are many more passages from the Bible that could be cited here. This "public" prophesying ceased with the death of St. John the Apostle, but since then there have been literally thousands of "private prophecies" from all sorts of Christian mystics and saints. The problem with private prophecy as it relates to the church is that no matter how beloved the saint or mystic, and even if they are approved for the acts of beatification, that does not mean the church has cited any prophecy as being authentic. It merely means that the writings have nothing in them contrary to Catholic doctrine.

Also, while studying private prophecy throughout the ages, one inevitably finds one saint after another contradicting each other. However, there are a few subjects where you can find prophecies from hundreds of different saints and mystics all basically saying the same thing. One subject has to do with the so-called Three Days of Darkness. One of the most popular of these comes from the Blessed Anna-Maria Taigi, who prophesied:

> God will send two punishments; one will be in the form of wars, revolutions and other evils; it shall originate on earth. The other will be sent from heaven. There shall come over the whole earth an intense darkness lasting three days and three nights. Nothing can be seen, and the air will be laden with pestilence which will claim mainly, but not only, the enemies of religion. It will be impossible to use any man-made lighting during this darkness, except blessed candles. He who out of curiosity opens his window to look out, or leaves his home, will fall dead on the spot. During these three days, people should remain in their homes, pray the Rosary, and beg God for mercy.[8]

---

8   Yves Dupont, *Catholic Prophecy: The Coming Chastisement* (Rockford, IL: T A N Books & Publishers, 1977), 44.

There isn't space here, but it is interesting to note that there are many private prophecies similar to this one that have been recorded by many famous saints and mystics. From examining the eschatological discourse as well as pertinent passages in scripture, Catholic theologians have come up with a number of "signs" that will precede the end of the world. There are many both in and out of the church who believe we are now experiencing the final signs, especially those who take a more liberal approach to interpreting the completion of each sign:

1. Universal preaching of the Gospel
2. Conversion of the Jews
3. Return of Henoch and Elias
4. A great apostasy
5. The reign of the Antichrist
6. Extraordinary disturbances in nature

It should be noted that there is much debate as to whether these signs have yet come to pass and/or how they are to be interpreted metaphorically. However, for Catholics, it may be wise to not expend too much energy trying to interpret prophecy, for when the end of the world is to come is known to God alone: "Of that day and hour no one knows, not even the angels in heaven, but the Father only" (Matthew 24:36).

nostradamus

Although not taken seriously by many modern intellectuals, Michel de Notredame—known by his Latinized name Nostradamus—is one of the best-known ancient forecasters of catastrophic earth changes. Many supporters of Nostradamus cite the fact that his psychic predictions must first be deciphered before they can be of use because he was intentionally vague and he deviously worded his predictions so as not to anger the authorities of his time. Nostradamus was working within the depths of magic and therefore constantly risked persecution as a sorcerer by the church.

No matter what is said of the man, he certainly led an interesting life, with his fair share of hardship. Born in France in 1503, his Jewish family was forcibly converted to Roman Catholicism, and that oppression may have helped fuel his desire for knowledge.

MICHEL NOSTRADAMUS.
Médecin,
Né à S.ᵗ Remy, en Provence, le 14 Décemb. 1503.
Mort le 2 juillet 1566.

Nostradamus: physician, prophet, astrologer, and humanitarian.
(Illustration courtesy of Victor Baines)

While quite young, he learned Hebrew, Greek, and Latin, while also studying mathematics and astrology. By the time he was thirty, Nostradamus was a fairly respected physician with a wife and two sons.

But tragedy would befall him by the loss of his family due to the plague. Further disaster came soon after, as we are told that he was accused of heresy due to a careless remark he made about the Virgin Mary. He did not appear for his trial, and for the next eight years he wandered through Italy as a fugitive. In 1544, he returned to France to help fight the plague, which he did with some success, and by 1547, he was both wealthy and famous from his unorthodox remedies. He married again, fathered six more children, and began to study astrology more rigorously. Nostradamus became recognized as the leading astrologer of his time, was knighted by the King of France, and was routinely hired by the rich and famous. His prophecies, published in 1555, will forever be what he is most noted for.

Researchers indicate that Nostradamus most frequently would gaze into a still, reflecting surface of water in a brass bowl in order to receive divine guidance in a trance state. He would speak his prophecies aloud and then later write them down in Latin to be finally translated into French verses.

Studying the riddling verses of Nostradamus is a daunting and sometimes frustrating task. But I have included him here simply because a summary of his predictions from the 1500s with regard to earth changes bear remarkable similarity to many other prophecies both before and after his time.

One such prophecy reads:

> There will be a solar eclipse more dark and gloomy than any since the creation of the world, except after the death of Christ. And it shall be in the month of October that a great movement of the globe will happen, and it will be such that one will think the gravity of the earth has lost its natural balance and that it will be plunged into the abyss and perpetual blackness of space. There will be portents and signs in the spring, extreme changes, nations overthrown, and mighty earthquakes. (Epistle to Henri II)

By examining large quantities of Nostradamus's predictions, some historians believe he was referring to the time period of AD 2000, when the universe will renew itself and a New Age will begin. Sound familiar?

Edgar Cayce (1877–1945). The "Sleeping Prophet" is one of the world's most documented psychics and founder of the Association for Research and Enlightenment, which to this day continues psychic research and education. (Photo used by permission of the Edgar Cayce Foundation.)

According to Nostradamus, the New Age will last a thousand years, during which humankind is given the opportunity to develop its Higher Self and to evolve into new levels of spiritual consciousness. After this time, dark forces will once again be released, but this time humankind will be better prepared and will finally leave behind our physical bodies and fully enter the spirit realm. Once this happens, the earth will have fulfilled its purpose and be destroyed. Our spirit will forever travel to new dimensions and universes, all the while continuing to learn and grow.

edgar cayce

Probably the best-known psychic to ever predict earth changes was the "sleeping prophet" Edgar Cayce. His "readings" have been studied by professional geologists, psychic enthusiasts, and the medical community for more than eighty years, beginning long before his death in 1945. As a young boy, Cayce demonstrated psychic abilities and was able to talk to deceased relatives. He also reportedly demonstrated to his parents that he could memorize every word in his spelling book—not by reading it, but rather by sleeping with his head on it. However, this gift apparently faded, as Cayce was a poor student who did not go further than the seventh grade in school.

After a rather normal childhood, at the age of twenty-four Cayce caught a nasty cold, lost his voice, and discovered the ability to answer questions in his sleep. Suffering from a paralysis of the throat that doctors were unable to treat, Cayce reportedly dealt with his medical condition himself while in his trance state. News spread of this feat, the *New York Times* carried the story, and from then on Cayce became known as a miracle man. Eventually Cayce founded the Association for Research and Enlightenment (A.R.E.), which is still dedicated to initiating research and educating the public on psychic phenomena.

In his time, Cayce gave more than 14,000 readings to over 8,000 people. He reportedly spoke on thousands of subjects, spoke in languages he hadn't learned, diagnosed medical conditions for people he had never met, and spoke fluently about past lives. But one of his most noted subjects is undoubtedly the metaphysics of our planet and human history. He also spoke of Atlantis as a real place, not a myth. Earth changes predicted by Cayce include:

- The Great Lakes will empty into the Gulf of Mexico.
- Most of Japan will go into the sea (become submerged).
- In the twinkling of an eye, northern Europe will be transformed as land submerges and the oceans roll in.
- New land will appear in the Atlantic and Pacific Oceans.
- The northern Atlantic coast on the United States will be dramatically altered, especially in New York and Connecticut; New York City will go under the sea.
- The southern parts and coastal regions of the Carolinas and Georgia will be submerged under the ocean.
- Some safe places to be in the United States: Ohio, Indiana, Illinois, and the Virginia Beach area, as well as southern and eastern Canada.

Cayce's predictions were to come to pass between the years 1958–1998, so obviously the predictions were wrong. But as far as this goes, Cayce is in good company. In the early 1970s, channeler Paul Solomon's predictions gained a lot of attention but never panned out. Like Cayce, Solomon's predictions included radical earth changes, such as Japan disappearing beneath the sea, the Great Lakes emptying into the Gulf of Mexico, and new continents rising in both the Atlantic and Pacific. Scientist and psychic Aron Abrahamsen also predicted massive earth changes would happen by the early '80s that never came to pass. And, more recently, Gordon-Michael Scallion—who reportedly receives his visions from his own Higher Self—predicted that a catastrophic fracture in the earth's crust would happen in California by 1993, and a second in Nevada, Oregon, and Arizona by 1998. The land mass to the west of this fracture would be inundated, and only isolated islands would survive. A very large seaport city would also be established in the Nebraska region, and Denver and Sedona would become coastal regions.

Why Were the Prophecies Wrong?

There can be many approaches to answering this question. Prophecy believers would argue that the Hopi, Mayan, Christian, and other prophecies are indeed coming to pass, and it's hard to argue that they are not. The first thing that I noticed about the predictions of Nostradamus, Cayce, and many other psychics is the fact that they never actually predict the end of the world, but rather the end of the world as we know it, with the dawning of a New Age of hope and community for all of humanity.

Secondly, it seems foolish for psychics to predict dates when things will happen. Where do these dates come from, and how accurate can they possibly be? In my personal experience, the planet, galaxy, and omniverse care not that we refer to a specific point in time by minute, hour, day, and year. And in the case of Nostradamus, whose predictions were made back in the 1500s, even if we give him only a 2 percent margin of error, that's about nine years, which would still leave time for many of his predictions to occur.

For Cayce and many other psychics, as well as the rest of the population who at times experience episodes of synchronicity, déjà vu, messages, visions, etc., we must consider where this information is coming from. At least two main sources must be cited: the subconscious of the person having the experience, and what Cayce himself has described as "the universal memory of nature," which can be compared to Jung's "collective unconscious" or, more recently, to Ervin László's version of the Akashic field.

If we are talking about psychic predictions being received from such an unconscious field, then we also must consider the social, economic, political, psychological, and physiological states of health or disease under which the human population is living during the time of these predictions. In this case, we should not be taking as direct precognitive experiences the predictions received by these psychics—or, for that matter, the prophecies of ancient people, saints, and mystics. For what seems to be going on is merely a reflection of the collective psyche being projected into the future. Apocalyptic prophecies can then be seen symbolically or metaphorically as possibilities for transformation, both at the levels of consciousness and physicality. And if that is true, then we still have a choice as to what lies ahead for our planet, which is what many spiritual leaders, as well as scientists, are now saying. So now, let's take a look at the science.

2012 Science:
Natural Disasters

Scientists tell us there is no doubt that this world is going to end. If it doesn't happen before, in about 5 billion years our sun will burn out, morph into a red giant, and turn the earth into a big cinder. That's science, and that's far in the future.

But what about right now? What real threats exist to our planet and way of life? Unfortunately, there is a fairly long list. Accelerating global warming, population explosion, and over 36,000 nuclear weapons do not bode well for the happy future of our species. Throw in the fact that many scientists believe we are overdue for the next volcanic super eruption, cataclysmic earthquake, or asteroid impact, and the future looks even bleaker.

Given these facts, it certainly seems that instead of our species being in its infancy (which in geological terms we certainly are), with many millions or even billions of years ahead of us to enjoy on this planet, the more likely probability is that the great human experiment may actually be coming to a rapid end.

However, after carefully reviewing the current facts of the matter, I can't help but feel cautiously optimistic. There seems to be no doubt that at some point in the future our species as we know it will cease to exist, but that may be a very long way off. The fact is that many "end of the world" prophecies and scientific models are simply not capable of what they predict. We now have a population of over 6 billion people on our planet, and it would be very hard at this point to wipe us all out. Sure, a major catastrophic event could severely reduce the human population and bring our technology-based civilization to its knees, but even if an event as big as the asteroid hit that wiped out the dinosaurs were to occur again, statistics predict that at least some of us would survive.

A survey of options that right now seem most likely, in order of nearest to furthest in time, might look something like this:

- The end of the world *as we know it* occurs as a result of either human-made technological or environmental disasters, or an extraterrestrial (asteroid or comet impact) or terrestrial (earthquake, volcano) event that deals our species a catastrophic but not lethal blow. This event would forever change our world but not extinguish our species.

- The human race will be extinguished by a natural or human-made disaster, but the planet will survive.
- Our planet will be destroyed by some catastrophic event, but we will have already moved into space, so at least some of our people will be saved.
- Our planet will be completely destroyed and our race annihilated if we are still on Earth when our sun goes nova in a few billion years.

Obviously it's the first two options that we should be concerned with at the moment, although other options have been recently proposed, such as humanity's "ascension" to a higher vibrational level, at which time we will leave this physical plane of existence, or that we miraculously will be saved from our crises by beings from another galaxy, among others. Although I am not one to discount any possibilities, it is my feeling that such options are not likely to happen in the next few years leading up to 2012. What is needed now is not some pie-in-the-sky wishful thinking. We, right now, have the capacity and the technology to help ourselves. It's time for us to grow up and accept responsibility for our actions and also prepare ourselves for those things that we can't control. So let's look at what those things might be.

Geologic events with the power to wipe out or severely devastate our entire civilization can be summarized by two categories: terrestrial and extraterrestrial.

TERRESTRIAL EVENTS:
- Volcanic eruptions
- Gigantic waves (tsunamis) caused by tectonic shifts
- Earthquakes

EXTRATERRESTRIAL EVENTS:
- Impacts from asteroids and comets
- Solar radiation or magnetic shifts of the sun

1980 VEI 5 eruption of Mount St. Helens. This is an oblique aerial view of the eruption of May 18, 1980, which sent volcanic ash, steam, water, and debris to a height of 60,000 feet. The mountain lost 1,300 feet of altitude and about ⅔-cubic mile of material. (Photo used courtesy of U.S. Geological Survey; photo by Austin Post, Skamania County, Washington.)

volcanic eruptions

Just ask the survivors of the 1991 eruption of Pinatubo in the Philippines or the dual eruptions of Tavurvur and Vulcan in Papua, New Guinea, in 1994 about hell on earth, and they will describe it for you. But even these terrible eruptions pale in comparison to a super eruption. On the Volcanic Explosivity Index (VEI), the Mount St. Helens blast of 1980 scored a 5. That size blast generally causes damage and suffering on a regional scale. The larger VEI 6 Pinatubo eruption of 1991 left hundreds of thousands of people homeless. But the largest eruption in historic time, the 1815 VEI 7 eruption of Tambora in Indonesia, spewed 150 times as much ash as Mount St. Helens, and an estimated 92,000 people lost their lives. About 10,000 direct deaths were caused by debris impacts, tephra fall, and pyroclastic flows (flows are fast-moving currents of hot gas, ash, and rock—collectively known as tephra—that can travel away from the volcano at up to 700 km/hour). An estimated 82,000 were killed indirectly in the aftermath by starvation, disease, and lack of clean water.

The VEI 7 eruption of Tambora was large enough to significantly change the weather across Europe and North America. The year 1816 became known as "the year without summer." However, geologic evidence suggests that even this eruption was miniscule when compared to the eruption at Yellowstone in Wyoming 2 million years ago, which left behind a crater eighty kilometers wide, or more recently, about 73,500 years ago, perhaps the largest explosion ever, the VEI 8 super eruption of Toba, in northern Sumatra, that is estimated to have ejected enough ash to bury the entire United States in ashen debris to a depth of close to a meter.

Many scientists believe that the after-effects of the super eruption in Toba were enough to cause ice age conditions in just a few months. The amount of sulfuric acid aerosols blown into the stratosphere was great enough to prevent 90 percent of normal sunlight from reaching the planet. There are even widely supported theories that this event nearly wiped out the human race, and that as little as a few thousand people may have survived. Without sufficient photosynthesis occurring on the planet, food sources for both humans and the animals they fed on were destroyed, and so our ancestors simply starved to death.

Now that we have recovered to over 6 billion souls on the planet, it seems unlikely that we would be reduced to only a few thousand again. But an eruption of this magnitude would certainly cause worldwide devastation and bring our consumer/industrial way of life to a screeching halt. The fact is that we are simply not prepared for the winter that would accompany such an event.

So what are the chances of a VEI 8 event happening in the near future? Well, we know that it has been over 70 millennia since the last event that large, so statistically speaking, we are due. And although evidence suggests that no significant eruptions have occurred in Yellowstone for 70,000 years, visiting the geysers, hot springs, and bubbling pools of mud assures us that there is hot magma very close to the surface. Who knows when or if Yellowstone will experience another super eruption. But we would be naïve to close our eyes to the geological evidence that these events seem to happen at approximately 650,000-year intervals, and we have already reached the next interval.

tsunamis

Many people don't know this, but while talking about volcanoes it's completely natural to talk about tsunamis because they can go hand in hand. A mechanism called volcano lateral collapse, such as what happened on a relatively small scale in 1792 to Japan's Unzen volcano, caused waves high enough to kill over 14,000 people. Now that is nowhere near the devastation caused by the earthquake-created tsunami in Indonesia that killed close to 300,000 people in 2004. But the really frightening thing is that there are ocean island volcanoes large enough that if they collapse could cause waves that make the Indonesian tsunami look small. Computer models show that the next volcano collapse in Hawaii is likely to generate tsunami waves as fast as a jumbo jet that will reach the United States in around twelve hours and destroy many of our great cities, along with many in Canada, Japan, and China.

An even more serious threat may be the Cumbre Viejo volcano in the Canary Islands. Researchers have discovered that a large portion of the volcano has detached itself and that this enormous chunk of rock will eventually crash into the sea. Nobody knows when it will happen, but when it does, some scientists predict the tsunami waves will reach skyscraper heights and pummel the metropolitan areas of Miami, Washington, Baltimore, New York, and Boston within nine hours. It is estimated that if this scenario were to happen now, the lack of massive evacuation procedures would leave tens of millions of people killed, and the physical devastation would be at a scale that would wipe out the insurance industry, and soon afterward a global economic crisis would affect the entire world.

earthquakes

Earthquakes are a daily occurrence on our planet; thousands are reported every day. In 2006 alone there were over thirty sizable quakes, and sixteen reportedly caused human fatalities for a total of around 7,000 reported deaths. But according to the U.S. Geological Survey, this was a relatively quiet year since historically there have been dozens of years when quakes claimed more than 50 thousand lives, and loss of life from the biggest earthquakes have been in the hundreds of thousands.

Geologists and seismologists warn that the rise of big cities along seismic fault lines will result in unprecedented catastrophes in the near future. Fatalities in the millions are projected if and when a large earthquake rocks one of the major cities on the planet.

In addition to loss of life, researchers are now warning that there could well be another significant factor to consider: the globalization of the world's economic structure makes many industrialized countries dependent on each other. So, for example, when the next big earthquake hits the island of Japan, which is an extremely unstable region rocked with daily small quakes, if Tokyo is severely affected, then many other countries, including the United States, will feel the impact on an economic level. In order to rebuild Tokyo, it is projected that the Japanese will have to sell off foreign investments and shut down production facilities in other countries. This would severely affect the global economy, especially the United States, and a depression as deep or even deeper than in the 1930s could be the consequence. With the population now much larger than the last great depression, and with the proliferation of weapons of mass destruction, a deep depression might be the trigger of another world war. The question right now isn't *if* Tokyo will be hit by a devastating earthquake—the question is when and what effects it will have on our way of life.

pole shift

Some scientists have theorized that as Earth hurtles through space at 1.3 million miles per hour, there is a chance that the North and South Poles of the planet could "move." This pole shift, also called axis shift or axis flip, would cause a radical displacement of

Identified NEO object–asteroid Ida, approximately 32 miles in length. (Photo: NASA)

Earth's axis of rotation and possibly cause the planet to flip end over end, or in another theory, a slippage of the planet's solid crust over the molten interior could cause the polar locations to change.

There is much debate as to whether this has happened in the past and/or if it will happen in the future. Interestingly enough, we can see descriptions similar to the effects of pole shift in both Hopi prophecies and in the Bible. Scientists believe that should this type of event occur, it would be a disaster of enormous proportions: giant tsunamis would cover the earth in water as the continents would shift under the oceans. Tremendous earthquakes would rock the planet as lava and poisonous gases would spew from the earth. Ash would fill the sky and obliterate the sun. All signs of life—including us—would be buried under deep debris and ice at the bottom of the oceans.

Pole-shift theorists provide a few broad categories of evidence supporting this concept:

ICE SHEETS: Small changes of Earth's orbital geometry over long periods of time, coupled with period changes of climate, do not explain the rapid appearance and disappearance of continental ice sheets. And they don't explain why during the last Ice Age the Hudson Bay area was covered in ice while the North Pole was ice free. Only rapid and dramatic changes could cause this.

UNEXPLAINED GLACIAL STRIATIONS: The claim here is that the slow continental drift and tectonic plate theory doesn't explain some glacial striations that seem to show opposite movement away from the poles instead of toward them.

THE FROZEN MAMMOTHS: There has been speculation that the ancient mammoth was not an Arctic species as currently believed, primarily because it didn't have the proper hide and it would not have been able to survive without vast amounts of vegetation, which the frozen Arctic couldn't provide. Yet there are thousands of mammoth skeletons frozen in the Arctic ice sheets. How did they get there?

NEAR-EARTH OBJECTS: It has been argued that possibly Venus or some other large mass passed close enough to Earth to cause either electromagnetic or gravitational shifts large enough to throw Earth out of rotation.

Barringer Meteor Crater in Arizona. The meteor impact produced a massive explosion about 150 times the yield of the atomic bombs used at Hiroshima and Nagasaki. (Photo: U.S. Geological Survey)

MAGNETIC SHIFTS: Magnetic minerals in sedimentary rocks
have been found to show that the North Pole had shifted
more than 50 degrees around 800 million years ago.

Many scientists don't believe the evidence thus far presented is enough to confirm catastrophic pole shifts. However, in light of ancient prophecies that seem to describe such events, coupled with the knowledgeable scientists that support the pole-shift theory as being real, it is enough to make one wonder about these ultimate disasters and if one is in our near future, as prophesied.

near-earth objects

Over the past forty years, scientists have discovered that many asteroids and comets have collided with Earth throughout its 4.5-billion-year history. The impact of these near-Earth objects (NEOs) with our planet would be catastrophic, and they represent a real hazard to humanity. NEOs are comets and asteroids that have been nudged by the gravitational attraction of nearby planets into orbits that allow them to enter Earth's neighborhood. Composed mostly of water and ice with embedded dust particles, comets originally formed in the cold outer planetary system, while most of the rocky asteroids have formed in the warmer inner solar system between the orbits of Mars and Jupiter.

In the United States, NASA has a congressional mandate to catalog all NEOs that are at least 1 kilometer (0.6 miles) wide. At this size and larger, an impacting NEO would cause catastrophic local damage and significant to severe global consequences. As of the close of 2006, over 4,400 near-Earth objects have been discovered; 855 of these NEOs are asteroids with a diameter of approximately 1 kilometer or larger. According to the most widely accepted projections, there are still 200 more of these that have not yet been found. The United States, European Union, and other nations are currently scanning for NEOs in an effort called Spaceguard. Currently, efforts are underway to use an existing telescope in Australia to cover the 30 percent of the sky that is not yet surveyed.

Testing the "Peacekeeper" missile system. Each line, were its warhead live, represents the explosive power of 25 Hiroshima-sized bombs. (Photo: http://en.wikipedia.org/wiki/Image:Peacekeeper-missile-testing.jpg)

Near-Earth asteroids are further classified by their orbits:

NEAs: Near-Earth asteroids

ATENS: Earth-crossing NEAs with semi-major axes smaller than Earth's (named after asteroid 2062 Aten)

- *Apollos*—Earth-crossing NEAs with semi-major axes larger than Earth's (named after asteroid 1862 Apollo)

- *Amors*—Earth-approaching NEAs with orbits exterior to Earth but interior to Mars (named after asteroid 1221 Amor)

So far, 824 NEOs have been classified as Potentially Hazardous Asteroids (PHAs). According to NASA, "since their orbital paths often cross that of Earth, cometary collisions with Earth have occurred in the past and additional collisions are forthcoming. It is not a question of whether a comet will strike Earth, it is a question of when the next one will hit. It now seems likely that a comet or asteroid struck near the Yucatan peninsula in Mexico some 65 million years ago and caused a massive extinction of more than 75 percent of Earth's living organisms, including the dinosaurs."[9] While NASA feels that the next large impact coming from outer space isn't likely for at least the next couple of hundred years, until the NEOs are mapped and their orbits are known, disaster could strike at any time.

Humanmade Disasters

Just a century ago, the topic of humanmade threats to the planet would scarcely have been necessary. But as we rapidly approach 2012, humanmade disasters may be the biggest threat to humanity that we have ever seen. While natural disasters are for the most part out of our control, we do have the power to eliminate the threats to our world that we are directly responsible for. Right now, it seems that the largest threat to the survival of humanity is humanity itself. While we all appreciate the level of comfort that our modern technology affords us, it's time that we take a hard look at the way we apply our knowledge, the way we treat our environment, and our relationships with all those that

9   http://neo.jpl.nasa.gov/faq/

share our planet. Here is a list of some of the major situations that are threatening our very way of life.

atmosphere and climate threats

GLOBAL WARMING: The human enterprise has gotten so large that we are now capable of dramatically altering the base molecular components of Earth's atmosphere, especially with greenhouse gases such as carbon dioxide. The results of global warming are staggering:

- Worldwide, almost all of the mountain glaciers are melting.
- Planetary temperatures are rising. As the oceans get warmer, storms and hurricanes get larger and more deadly.
- Forest systems are being destroyed by beetles and other insects as global warming disrupts the delicate balance of nature.
- Coral reefs, which are vital to the health of ocean species, are dying at an alarming rate.
- Sea levels are rising and displacing many coastal peoples. Projections indicate this could affect many large cities and billions of people around the world in the near future.

AIR POLLUTION: Harmful levels of particulate matter, ozone, and sulfur dioxide cause disease from respiratory infections, heart disease, and lung cancer. In 1997, WHO joined with the World Resources Institute (WRI) and others to estimate that, annually, nearly 700,000 deaths are related to air pollution and that about 8 million avoidable deaths will occur worldwide by 2020.[10]

UV RADIATION: Depletion of the ozone layer aggravates the health effects of ultraviolet radiation from the sun. Melanoma and non-melanoma skin cancers, as well as cataracts, are increasing yearly.

DROUGHTS AND HEAVY RAINFALL: As climate change is increasing, the amount of areas experiencing severe droughts is rising. At the

---

10 "Working Group on Public Health and Fossil-Fuel Combustion," *Lancet* 350 (1997), 1341.

same time, when dry areas do receive rain, it is coming harder and stronger, causing massive erosion, flooding, and loss of life.

warfare threats

WEAPONS OF MASS DESTRUCTION: These are available to many countries. There are currently more than 30,000 nuclear warheads worldwide. Small arms, mines, and grenades are proliferating as well.

POVERTY: Lack of food and drinking water is now causing both civil wars and wars between countries. As population numbers continue to increase and resources continue to diminish, this will get worse before it gets better.

TERRORISM: As the gap between rich and poor continues to increase, and political and religious fanaticism prevails, terrorism will continue to be a chosen option instead of peaceful resolutions.

health threats

RESISTANCE TO ANTIBIOTICS: Misuse and overuse of antibiotics since the 1960s have created MDRs (Multiple Drug Resistant bacteria), which pose multiple and widespread health-care problems.

SICK CITY SYNDROME: High crime, social unrest, growing strains on roads and public transport, educational underachievement, lack of green space, dense populations, and new strains of airborne diseases in indoor environments all threaten our cities.

STRESS: The quickened demands of industrial lifestyles cause chronic activation of stress hormones, leading to serious psychological and physiological maladies.

SLEEP DEPRIVATION: Stress, worry, depression, noise, not allowing enough time for sleep, and medical problems cause medical and psychological disorders as well as an increase in accidents.

NOISE POLLUTION: Excessive human- and machine-made noise has been proven to detrimentally affect hearing, cardiovascular health, and cognitive performance, leading to increased annoyance that contributes to social unrest and crime.

CONTAGIOUS DISEASES: Over 25 million people have died of AIDS so far. New and previously unknown diseases are surfacing throughout the globe due to numerous humanmade factors:

- Encroachment on wildlife habitats by new housing and commercial construction brings people into contact with animals and the microbes they harbor.

- Changes in agriculture practices attract new crop pests and the microbes they carry to farming communities, exposing people to unfamiliar diseases.

- Destruction of rainforests by building roads through forests and clearing areas for settlement or commercial ventures causes people to encounter insects and other animals harboring unknown microorganisms.

- Rapid growth of cities, especially in developing countries, concentrates large numbers of people in crowded areas with poor sanitation, which fosters the transmission of contagious diseases.

- Global warming affects cities and urban areas by keeping insects alive that would otherwise not be able to survive in the winter.

- Modern transportation vehicles ship cargo that harbors insects and rats that can spread diseases to faraway destinations.

- International jet-airplane travel can carry people infected with a new disease to the other side of the world before their first symptoms even appear.

- Malnutrition and chemical pollutants make people more susceptible to disease.

- Overuse of chemical fertilizers make algae grow in rainwater, which forms breeding pools for mosquitoes that transmit diseases.

POISONS: Our environments are now riddled with toxic quantities of lead, sulfuric acid, mercury, asbestos, insecticides, dioxins, formaldehyde from plastics, chlorinated hydrocarbons, and PCBs, among numerous others.

sustenance threats

WATER THREATS:

- Rain has become poisonous, with toxic levels of nitrates, sulfates, and sulphur dioxide.
- Aquifers, groundwater, and rivers, especially near industrial and chemical farming areas, are severely polluted, and drinkable water is becoming scarce.
- Many urban areas depend on water being piped and canalled in from long distances. As drinkable water becomes more and more scarce, these cities will suffer massive shortages.
- Currently, about 40 percent of the human population, over 2 billion people, have no access to clean water or sanitation.
- As the human population continues to increase, industrial, agricultural, and individual water demands escalate and cannot possibly be met.
- The oceans of our world are being contaminated and put into poor health by toxic wastes, oil spills, garbage dumping, wastewater, acid rain, and global warming, among other factors.

FOOD THREATS:

- As the fertility of croplands continues to diminish and adding more fertilizers makes a bad situation worse, food prices will continue to escalate, which will cause more hunger and suffering.
- Rapid globalization of food production and trade has increased the potential for international incidents involving food contamination with microbial or chemical hazards.
- Genetic modification of food and seeds reduces genetic diversity, making them more vulnerable to disease and pests. This furthers

the need for pesticides (often created by the same companies creating and promoting genetically engineered crops).

- Food distribution to urban areas is completely dependent on fossil fuels. When transportation of goods is disturbed for any reason, people will go hungry, and social unrest and disputes will escalate.
- As urban sprawl continues, less and less farmland is available.

Since the time of the Industrial Revolution in the mid-1800s—less than one century ago—the human enterprise has gotten so large that it now threatens the very survival of life on our planet. Have we reached the point of no return to the world as we know it? *Time* magazine recently reported that we have. "Earth Is at the Tipping Point," declared the cover of the April 3, 2006, edition. Elders of many tribes, national leaders, and scientists from around the world have been saying the same thing for years.

Will the human species wake up in time? That appears to be the biggest question we have ever faced.

Part Two:
The First Shamans Speak

Chapter 3

TIME AND OUR ROLE AS CO-CREATORS

"Grandfather, many people are saying that we can save the world if we change our level of consciousness, while other people are saying it's too late because the immensity of our human project has gotten so large that it will be swiftly and painfully corrected by some sort of apocalypse. Still others are saying that there is nothing wrong. How do I sort this all out?"

That is for you to decide, hijo. But I will comment. Let's begin with the third category of people you mentioned, the ones who see nothing wrong. These people are simply hypnotized by materialism. We will speak more of that later. The other two groups have exactly the same mission right now.

"But how can that be, Grandfather? One group seeks to raise consciousness and the other group says forget about it—that the end is coming. How can they have the same mission?"

Because both scenarios require a state of consciousness that is not ordinary to what you have now. Those that are already aware of the need in a consciousness change for the health of humanity are already seeking ways of cultivating non-ordinary states. These non-ordinary states will become ordinary in your future, but right now they are a minority. These states include heightened compassion for all life, feelings of unity, and letting go of self-centeredness and the illusion of material possessions for happiness. Many possibilities exist if the second group is correct and it is too late for humanity to wake up in time. But in all cases, if this were to happen, you would still need the same thing. Survival for many will depend on the compassion of others. In order to help each other survive, you will all need to change into more loving and caring beings that are not tied to your materialistic view of the world. This knowledge I am sharing with you is very liberating. It shows you that in both scenarios the need for a transformation in human consciousness is coming. So don't worry about the outcome. Live in the now and begin your transformation right away.

"I haven't thought about it that way; thank you, Grandfather!"

Do not thank me, hijo. There is much work to be done. The first thing I suggest is that you alter your view of time.

"Yes, I have been learning about that. People are now saying that we must move away from our Gregorian calendar and tune in to galactic time. Do you agree with that?"

Yes. Absolutely. As you know, your calendar is the basis of your civilization. It was forced onto the world by the Catholic Church for human-centered reasons. For control. And this church destroyed the usage of other sacred calendars, which were given to the people that it conquered. Now it is all about business. Human business. This calendar involves the rotation of only your planet and your sun, which makes it a tiny calendar in the midst of a huge omniverse. To expand your consciousness, you must enlarge your view to look beyond your watch and your Gregorian calendar to agree with other people what day and time it is. That you call today Tuesday means nothing to me. It means nothing to your Mother or your Grandmother.

"So what is important, Grandfather?"

Consciousness is important. Creation is important. You must begin to see yourself in proportion to where you are in creation and consciousness. When your calendar is based on actions that are in tune with creation and consciousness, you will be free from the stress of how much you can produce in a workday. When your consciousness is in tune with creation, you will be at one with the omniverse. Right now, your consciousness is speeding faster and faster away from the consciousness of your Mother and your Grandmother. This is why you have forgotten their faces.

"Is this why time seems to be speeding up?"

Time is not speeding up, hijo. It is the mind of your people that is speeding up. But your mind is not your consciousness. Your mind is what allows you to make decisions, but right now your mind is based entirely on this silly calendar of human business that means nothing to the omniverse or creation. Your consciousness is much larger than your silly calendar. Your consciousness is creation, which includes all. Step out of your human-centered view of the world and you will see this. You will see how narrow your mind is.

"But Grandfather, it really does feel to me like time is speeding up. Why is that?"

It is because your mind is speeding up. Everything that surrounds the life of your people is speeding up. Just in the blink of an eye, your people went from writing on clay tablets to emailing across the globe—from walking to flying. Every day you are discovering another way to go faster. It is hard for your mind to keep up the pace. Actually, it is already far behind, and that is why you feel so much stress. Your mind cannot keep up with a computer. Your creations have already passed the speed of your mind. But listen, hijo, you already know all of this. What is it that you really want to ask me?

"I guess I would ask you, then, what is time?"

Now that is a good question. You perceive the things that are happening to you now as being present. And all other events that you believe to be real—events that happen to you or anyone else—you regard as past, present, or future. But maybe the positions that you regard as past, present, and future are all a product of your mind, not your consciousness. Suppose your consciousness has no past, present, or future. Then, the only thing you could really say about time is that time involves change. You can say that something remains unchanged through time, but there could be no time if nothing changed. It is the rate of change that your mind is experiencing that is causing you to feel like time is speeding up.

"So it's just an illusion that things appear to be moving faster?"

No, hijo, it's not an illusion. Human creation is definitely moving faster. Every day you invent machines that produce more, computers that go faster, new ways of communicating electronically. All the while, the rest of creation is moving at a different speed. That speed is increasing too, but at a rate much slower than the rate that humans are creating.

"I don't understand, Grandfather."

The hectic pace of modern life: Interstate 80 outside of Berkeley, California. (Photo: http://en.wikipedia.org/wiki/Image:I-80_Eastshore_Fwy.jpg)

Think of it this way. Just in your short lifetime, you have seen the invention of the cell phone. Quickly after that everyone seems to have one. Quickly after that you could send pictures, now you can send email and surf the Internet from your mobile phone. It is all moving faster and faster— who knows what will come next? But look outside your window to that tree that grows. Is that tree growing faster now than when you were a kid? Does the robin sitting on the branch fly faster than its parents did? Does it still take nine months for a human pregnancy? You see, hijo, what is speeding out of control is what humans are creating—including the species itself. Every day, the speed at which the human population grows is increasing. Soon it will be more than your Mother can bear. Humans are out of sequence to that which your Mother can provide. So what must be corrected is the silly need to go faster, to always produce more than yesterday.

"If I hear you correctly, it is that we are taking more from our Mother than she can produce, is that correct?"

Of course, hijo. You take oil from the ground much faster than oil can be created. You take trees faster than they can be created. You are out of balance with creation.

"What can be done, Grandfather?"

Stop your destructive compulsion to create faster than your Mother! Get back in tune with creation. Synchronize your time, your rate of material change, back to the time of your Mother. Change your mind. Be aware of being aware of your consciousness, not only your mind! Change your concept of time away from the rate of change in what humans can produce and toward the change and evolution of the level you are aware of consciousness.

"But how is this done?"

Your Mother is experiencing herself in relation to galactic and omniversal time, just as an insect that lives only for weeks or months experiences time differently than a whale that lives to be a hundred years old. Humans that are in touch with their Mother may also experience the passage of time as it relates to the galaxy and omniverse. Humans also have the capacity to experience time through the actions of creation as they pertain to human consciousness. This was known to human cultures such as the Maya. They did not experience time through the Gregorian calendar or by how many goods they could produce during a revolution of the earth around the sun. Their temporal reality was based on cycles of creation. Reviving this knowledge would be a good starting point for your people. But understand that your mind is aware of many things that they were not, so you must add those acts of creation for your view to be complete.

"I'm not sure of what you're suggesting, Grandfather."

What I'm suggesting is to align your daily actions to the acts of creation as they apply to human beings and also to your Mother, who provides you with life. In doing so, you will at the same time align with actions of creation in the grander temporal scheme of your galaxy and omniverse. Open your mind and your consciousness to the actions of creation that govern human life, not only those actions created by human minds, which is your main focus now. These actions of creation are actions that you might call spiritual, but not religious.

"Yes, I have come to understand the differences between spiritual actions and religious actions. Spiritual actions are of a personal nature, while religion is more collective."

That is true, hijo, but there is more to it than that. The time has come for each of your people to claim their own connection with the spiritual aspects of human life. Religions were founded through the non-ordinary experiences of their prophets. But in the face of the human mind speeding away from its Mother, you are now being asked not to simply follow the directives received from the prophets but rather to experience non-ordinary states of consciousness yourself so that you can be guided by your own experiences, not the experiences of others. Direct connection to spiritual actions of creation through non-ordinary experiences is what is required now—such is what you are experiencing in this moment while 'speaking' to me.

"OK. I think I understand what you are asking, but I'm still not clear about what you mean by aligning with acts of creation as applied to human beings."

Acts of creation for a butterfly include life as a larva, pupa, butterfly, and, finally, acts of reproduction. Acts of creation for a pine tree include sprouting from a seed, growing toward the sun, dropping pine cones, and, finally, merging with the soil of the Mother. Human acts of creation include many more experiences, due to their self-reflective nature. Core experiences include breathing and reproducing, but your complex organism also allows you to experience feelings and emotions, intuition, and the consciousness of being aware that you are aware. These are but a few actions—it will be better for you to inventory these actions of creation for yourself rather than just receiving a list from me. But I will tell you that all of these acts of creation are pulses of creation that you can align with in a way that turns your lifestyle away from the business calendar and toward a more conscious way of life. I suggest you study the

alignment of the Maya toward actions of creation and then add the experience of your people.
When you have done this, you will then be at a new starting point for discovering non-ordinary
states of consciousness and what can be learned from there.

"Thank you, Grandfather, I will do my best."

<hr/>

At this point, I spent a great deal of time learning more about the Mayan calendars and the actions of creation that they imply. What I found was fascinating, especially when discovering what needed to be added to the Mayan view of time and creation so that I could have a conscious connection to the actions of creation applicable to our "now." This will be explained in more detail in Part 3 when discussing practical uses of the Mayan creation calendar. For now, let's just say that in understanding "actions of creation" as spoken by Grandfather Fire, the human experiences of equality, harmony, instinct, mortality, accomplishment, potential, independence, desire, joy, family, freedom, production, loneliness, sacrifice, thought, intuition, change, guidance, destiny, creation, and preparation, among many others, all play a vital role in the shifting of human consciousness that we are being asked to achieve.

Living in the Now

In my study and practice of shamanism, as well as my study and practice with the calendar of creation, I began to notice two important things pertaining to the transformation in consciousness spoken to me by the First Shamans. The first is that shamanic practices can be used by anyone; they are not limited to those given the title "shaman" by a community. In a shamanic community, there are many occasions when even though the shaman is doing the work of healing, blessing, divining, or offering, the community is also participating in the ceremony or ritual, so in those moments everyone is involved in shamanic practice.

For those of us who do not live in a community or setting where shamanic practices are used in a central role that guides daily life, we can still use shamanic practices for defined purposes. When using shamanic practices, we generally are seeking a particular outcome for our actions. When I enter an altered state and converse with the First Shamans, I am seeking a particular outcome: the gleaning of knowledge pertaining to my questions. A Wirrarika shaman enters a trance state to connect with spirit guides and send messages to the ocean, asking for rain, or to a particular deity, asking for spiritual energy to be used in healing.

But of equal importance is how entering these states of consciousness alters our actions in our daily lives. In this way—in altering our worldview—our daily lives acquire a flavor that can be more accurately described as mystical rather than shamanic. A mystic can be described as a person who lives a life of unity with all beings, one who transcends the dominating aspects of ego and realizes the oneness of all.

What I have realized is that even though shamanic practices designed to have a certain outcome are vitally important and develop our ability to enter non-ordinary states, of equal value is how we integrate our experiences of altered states into our everyday lives so as to alter the way we live. That is the path of the mystic. And for those of us not living in a community supported by a shamanic worldview, i.e., mainstream Western culture, this is an important distinction to be made. For those of us engaged in shamanic practices but not looked at by our community as being shamans, what we are really doing when we strive for health and compassion in our daily lives is the blending of shamanic practices with a mystical worldview. The path of the mystic is all about how we are living right now—which is exactly what the calendar of creation, as well as the other practical applications of the First Shamans' teachings, are leading us to do: living in the now. This is the topic I asked Grandfather Fire about next.

"Abuelo, please tell me about the importance of living in the now, because I have found this to be a core teaching in what you have guided me to learn."

The first key in what you are asking about is to understand the difference between passive reflection and self-absorption. You can live in the now, as you say, while being completely self-absorbed, or you can live in the now while being passively reflective. There is a big difference in those two states of consciousness. You have been taught to be self-absorbed, to strive for your own happiness and the happiness of a few others that are close to you. But when you are passively reflective, you see yourself and your actions as pertaining to the larger web of life. Then you can see yourself for who you truly are, not simply as what you imagine yourself to be.

"Can you tell me how this works?"

You must passively view yourself as if you were watching your thoughts and actions through the eyes of your Grandmother, the First Shaman. Watch yourself through the eyes of your

Grandmother as if you are watching someone else. Do not judge what you see. Simply stand aside and watch the effects of fear or joy, loneliness or intuition. When you can do this, you will be ready for the next step.

"I understand the difference between self-absorption and passive reflection. But why do you say to watch myself from the eyes of my Grandmother?"

You already know this, hijo, you just have not thought about it this way before. As a result of your years spent visiting and connecting to the spirits of nature, do you not feel them watching you now as you live your life?

"Yes, Grandfather, I have felt that for many years. The trees and plants, animals and insects, even you and my Mother, the clouds and the sun—I feel all of you watching me and what I am doing. Because of this, my life has changed dramatically."

That is what I am talking about! That is what you need to teach your people. When they can feel the spirits watching them, they will see that they are accountable for their actions—accountable to their Grandmother. This is not about judgment or blame for previous actions, no. This is about seeing yourself through the eyes of your Grandmother right now. In every moment, see from her eyes, see what you are doing. See if your actions are in line with her actions. Ask yourself: am I helping her in her tasks of creation or am I destructing what she is creating? This way of living in the now joins your actions with the actions of your Grandmother Growth and Mother Earth.

"I understand, Grandfather. But I have already been sharing this teaching, not quite the same way as you have just shared with me, but in a similar way, with thousands of people for many years. And the mystics of my people have been saying this same sort of thing for much longer. Why is it so hard for people to use this knowledge?"

It is because you secretly think that you already know the answers to your personal problems. First you have to truly admit that you don't know all the answers. Then you must humbly surrender control and seek the truth. Listen carefully to this, hijo, because it is vital: transformation in consciousness is directly proportional to the amount of TRUTH you can handle.

"Yes. I think I see what you are saying now. Teachers such as Gurdjieff, Ouspensky, and others have been promoting self-observation as an instrument for change and awakening for a long time, but what you are saying is different, bigger."

That is right, hijo, the old ways are not enough anymore. As the mind of your people speeds faster and faster away from your Mother, you are being asked to do more. It is not just about self-realization anymore. It's about awakening to something much larger. It is about co-creating with your Mother and Grandmother. Of course, right now you are already co-creating with them by simply being alive, but what we are talking about here is intentional co-creation—the melding of your actions with theirs in order to restore harmony and balance between humans and the rest of the world.

But seeing through the eyes of your Mother is not easy for your people right now because their mind is headed in other directions. It is hard for them to accept the truth because the knowledge of the truth would then require radical change.

"I have noticed that people are afraid of change. It's much easier to simply keep up the assumption that there's nothing wrong with our culture or to admit we need change but to keep putting it off until tomorrow. Even though many people realize the necessity for change, it's hard to give up the comforts we are so used to—even though we know they cannot last much longer."

This is all based on fear, hijo. One of the biggest fears of your people is the fear of nothing happening. You gauge your life by accomplishments, your work by how much you can produce. It is okay to just BE, hijo. There is no need to feel anxious because you feel you should always be accomplishing something. One of the problems is that you never know what that something is. Once you have something, you want something else. Inner and outer peace is accomplished when you are unafraid of nothing happening. When this fear is vanquished, you open the door to seeing yourself as you truly are, not by what you have or what you accomplish. You live in the now, not the past or the future.

Our Personal Role in the Transformation of Human Consciousness

Many of us are now asking the question, "What am I to do?" We ask this as we begin to feel unsatisfied with our lives or when we wake up to the reality that there must be more to life than how much we can produce. A growing number of people are feeling restless about the future; some are even in a state of downright panic. I asked our Grandfather about this.

Listen closely, hijo: the best thing that can happen to your people right now is for all of them to become disillusioned, disappointed, disheartened. These feelings are what precede awakening. The more sick and tired you are of the way things are, the more energy you will give toward transformation! Are you feeling dissatisfied? Restless? Disappointed? Or feeling ungratified by money, possessions, success, status? Good! This is the first step to waking up to your True Self!

"I understand the wisdom of what you say, Grandfather, but for those of us who feel this way, what are we supposed to do?"

Tell your people not to be afraid of what will happen to them if they abandon their old ways. The old ways must be abandoned in order to change. When, during the course of the day, you begin to feel worried about the changes you are making or planning, simply turn your mind toward passive reflection and see yourself and your actions through the eyes of your Grandmother. If your actions are in tune with hers, there is absolutely nothing to worry about. Negative feelings are caused by you, not by what happens to you. You will always react to external happenings, but it is how you react that is the key to happiness and peace.

"So you're saying it's okay to have these feelings of dissatisfaction?"

Yes! It's an important part of your process in awakening. But you must be careful not to dwell on these shadow feelings. The shadow is the partner of light. But as children of the sun, it is your job to spread the light. Do not secretly take pleasure in negativity. It is a trap that people often fall into. People often secretly enjoy their own depression, and they can hardly wait to tell you about it. Shadow emotions like jealousy or anger can give one a false sense of aliveness. You are human, so at times these emotions may arise. But don't live there. As much as you can, in every moment, walk the earth as a little sun. As you do this, you will break free from the spell that has captured your people. You must dare to think for yourself! Do not give your power over to other people! Arrange your life so that your actions are in line with your Mother. That is your task right now.

"Grandfather, you say not to worry about what will happen if we give up our old ways. But many of us have spent a lifetime building what we have. Are we to just turn our backs on all those things? That is scary to even think about, let alone do."

Learn from what you have accomplished, hijo. Everything has a purpose. But recognize that even with all you have done, you still feel like there is more. That is good. Do not turn your back, look forward. But remember—and this is important—anything that you struggle too much for, you will be afraid of losing. There is no point in worrying about money, prestige, or how other people see you. Align your acts of creation with your Mother, and everything else will fall into place. You will know what to do next.

"Are you talking about intuition?"

Yes, hijo! Now you are understanding. Intuition is alignment. What you call synchronicity is alignment. When you begin to know your True Self, your Luminous Self, you no longer must struggle to make good things happen. They just do! The more you are in alignment with your Mother, the more intuition and synchronicity become normal acts of creation for you that you feel all the time. Your Luminous Self does not need exterior success to validate your worth or to make you happy. It is good to create things, things in alignment with your Mother, but do not fall into the trap of judging your worth on what you produce. Spread the light, and the results of your actions will come naturally from your heart—from your Luminous Self.

"But Grandfather, many people want to know what their specific task or job is to be during these times of transformation. What can you tell me about that?"

Yes, everyone has talents, knowledge, and skills, whether they know them or not, and everyone has one or more specific tasks to contribute in these times of radical change. This is a big subject, hijo, which we will speak of more later. First we must speak of something else. In order for your people to find their true tasks that are in alignment with their Mother, they must awaken to the Luminous Self. It is only from this state of consciousness that the guidance of unity and alignment become clear.

Chapter 4

Transformation Through Uniting with Our Luminous (True) Self

"Abuelo, please tell me more about the Luminous Self."

The Luminous Self is the eternal self. The divinity inside man, the kingdom of heaven, unity with creation. When you sense there is something more, something else beyond the ordinary routines of your life, this is the Luminous Self seeking to awaken.

"Awaken from what, Grandfather?"

Your people are psychically asleep, hijo. Even with the world crumbling around them, they continue to maintain that they are not asleep, that they are perfectly conscious beings. This is madness! Even those that are beginning to awaken, those that are starting to see again the face of their Mother, need to become fully awake so that they can see and act from the truth.

"I don't quite understand."

The degree to which you are awake to your Luminous Self can be measured by the degree to which you are able to accept the truth, especially a truth that your self-centered idea of yourself doesn't want to hear.

"What are these truths that we don't want to hear, Grandfather?"

Ah, hijo, for your people there are thousands. Too many to spell out for you. Let's stay on the topic of the Luminous Self first. The truth is that the Luminous Self is not your name, your home, your car, your career, or even the beliefs you hold. These are simply attachments. The truth is that you are asleep to your Luminous Self. You become upset when things go "wrong," your mechanical habits are almost impossible to break but equally difficult to endure. So you harbor feelings of resentment, you are easily antagonized, and you are unconsciously full with fear.

Would you like some more truth?

"No, I think that is enough for now, Grandfather."

Ha! I don't think so, hijo. How about one more? This is a good one—the truth is that every human being can awaken to their Luminous Self. Awareness of the Luminous Self is your sacred inheritance as human beings! But you have little chance of knowing that you are psychically asleep to your Luminous Self until you begin to awaken. When you are deeply asleep, it is hard for you to hear someone whispering to you to wake up.

"So how do we do it?"

I have already told you, hijo, the first step is to sense that there is something very wrong. It is like when you are having a bad dream and something inside of you tells you to wake up. Waking up to the Luminous Self is like awakening from a bad dream. This sense of the need to awaken is the sense that there is a way out from the bad dream that has hypnotized your people. Until your people begin to sense the need to awaken from the dream, nothing will change. This truth must be told at all costs, no matter how unpopular it may be. Listen, hijo: the more people whispering into the sleeping man's ear, the more probable he will awaken.

"Why do you say people are hypnotized, Grandfather?"

The Luminous Self experiences the truth NOW. Hypnotized people merely repeat what they are told.

"Yes, it does seem that my culture has been hypnotized by materialism, corrupt churches, and profit-at-all-cost corporations that influence the government. We are constantly being fed new things to make us happy, but in the end we are simply doing as we are told."

You are understanding this well; however, I hear a tinge of shame in your voice, hijo. This is important, so pay close attention: when you awaken to the Luminous Self, you break free from previous guilt and shame because you clearly see that those actions causing you grief were committed by a confused, misled, and asleep self who WAS NOT the real you.

"So when we awaken, we are absolved from our previous actions?"

Absolution is such a sticky word, hijo. It reeks of religious overtones. Let us not speak in terms of religion, philosophy, or psychology. These are just terms expressing human concepts. What I am speaking of is all these things and none of them at the same time.

When you awaken to your Luminous Self, feelings of guilt and shame are no longer relevant because you live squarely in the now. Not the past. Not the future. Where once you lived running around to and fro in the valley of darkness, now you stand atop the highest hill, overlooking all. You may see your previous actions below you while you lived in the valley, but you learn from them without judgment. You see that when you were running from one thing to another, you were hypnotized by the collective dream of a culture that has taken a wrong turn. The first step is acknowledging that you have lost the path of your Mother. Understanding this is what is important—moving forward while fully awake is what is imperative.

On the Sharing of Truth and Knowledge

"Grandfather, my process of awakening has shown me that I am to be of service to others during this time of transformation. I would hear what you have to say to me and others that have received this call."

It is good that you ask about this, hijo. It is a sign of humbleness that you don't pretend to know all the answers. The most important aspect of sharing with others is that you are awake yourself! The Luminous Self will then naturally be sharing in the spirit of co-creating with your Mother. When people that are still sleeping or are only partially awake think that they can heal others, great harms are done.

"What harms do you speak of, Abuelo?"

People who are hypnotized only repeat what they are told. This perpetuates the hypnosis; it helps to hypnotize others. Transforming into more compassionate beings who are awake to the truth will not be done by those who are still completely entranced. These people who are still asleep—or worse, those who are only partially awake—who are teaching others are simply evading their own healing. They are ignoring the whispering they hear to fully awaken, the need to heal and awaken themselves first. You will know these people because when you tell them this truth, they will become angry and insist that they are not asleep. Your culture is full of these false prophets, hijo.

"Yes, I have seen this many times for myself. There are thousands upon thousands of self-appointed teachers and 'masters' that have not awakened to the Luminous Self. They have not yet passed through the storm of awakening and therefore only serve to hypnotize others with their teachings."

You must make it clear to your people that only when you see yourself for who you truly are can you see others for who they really are and not what you want them to be. Hypnotized people want to hypnotize others so that they agree with them. Awakened teachers have no such agendas. Teachers who have not passed through disillusionment, disappointment, anxiety, and fear in order to fully awaken to the Luminous Self can only teach about how to go even deeper asleep. An awakened teacher will simply smile with acknowledgment when confronted with the actions of his previously sleeping self. A person still hypnotized will defend.

"Yes, Abuelo, I have learned that we can deal wisely with others only to the extent that we deal wisely with our self."

That is truth. And that is what it is all about. Your people must be willing with all their being to accept the truth, no matter how painful. When you see yourself through the eyes of your Mother, what you see is a hypnotized culture that is destructing what your Mother is creating. You also see how you truly feel about others. You see how much of your time you spend as an actor trying to convince people of who you are, persuade them to like you, persuade yourself even to like yourself. It takes much courage to realize this truth. Awakened teachers know this because they have passed through it.

"So as a person awakens, it is necessary to face and embrace the personal pain and global crisis that our asleep selves have created?"

It is the awareness of being able to observe your previous actions and then feel and work through the pain and shame of what you see that will help you to fully awaken. Without passing through this crisis, you cannot align with your Luminous Self, nor will you be able to teach others anything but how to become awakened. That is the simple truth, hijo.

Compassionate service to others of your own kind and aligning with the acts of creation of your Mother is what the Luminous Self is called to do. Service is key, and your Grandmother will have more to say to you about this topic. For right now, simply understand that to face the crises that the sleeping self has created is imperative, and one cannot heal others until this truth is embodied and worked through so that the Luminous Self emerges. Right now, both your personal and global crises are your doors leading to the Luminous Self.

Chapter 5

Understanding Earth Changes and Our Role

Grandmother Speaks on the Rise of the Feminine

"Grandmother, I would hear what you have to say about what is happening to our Mother Earth and what we can do about it."

Would you have me speak plainly, hijo?

"Yes, of course, Grandmother."

Good. Then let us start with a different question. Tell me, hijo, in your work are there more men or women that participate?

"Clearly there are more women, Grandmother."

Can you explain why?

"I believe it is because women are generally more open to accepting the need for change in our society."

At this moment, that is truth. Now that you know that, you must look at this situation in a much bigger way than you ever have before. Are you ready to listen and learn with an open heart, hijo?

"Yes, Grandmother, I have been preparing my whole life for this."

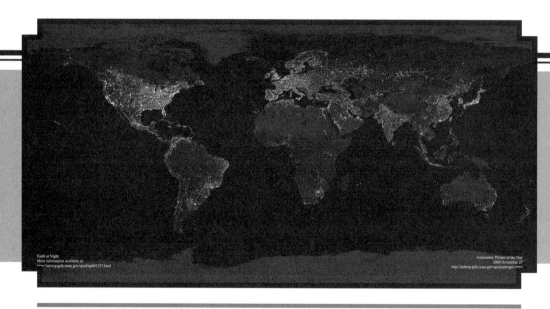

Earth at Night
More information available at:
http://antwrp.gsfc.nasa.gov/apod/ap001127.html

Astronomy Picture of the Day
2000 November 27
http://antwrp.gsfc.nasa.gov/apod/astropix.html

This composite of hundreds of photos taken from satellites displays the enormity of the human enterprise. (Image: NASA)

Good. And it is also good that you are nurturing your garden, hijo. It is good that you even have a garden. You have no particular talent for gardening. I don't say that to discourage you; on the contrary, I am very proud of you and expect you to keep working with the soil of your Mother and continue learning.

But listen, hijo, there is also another way for you to help your Mother's garden grow: nurture the women of your people. Your women must be allowed to plant new seeds into the minds of your people. Your garden is full of weeds. These weeds are the powerful men that have been hypnotized by their power. They are destroying your Mother. They must be pulled up so that new seeds can be planted and grown. These seeds must come from the women and the men equally. Men must no longer be allowed to dominate. This is imbalance. Balance must be restored, or there will be even greater suffering by all beings that share your world. Great tragedy will be upon you very soon if you do not heed these words!

"Please tell me more, Grandmother!"

First of all, this idea that there is one MALE god that sits above all else, an idea that is dominant in your culture, is at the core of the crises of your people. This immature view of reality, that God is an Authoritarian Father, has historically caused, and continues to perpetuate, the empowerment of men and the devaluation of women. Seeing God as the Father is completely imbalanced, for there can be no Father without a Mother. Masculine and feminine are a sacred pair. They are equals. This truth must be put back in balance on your world. The feminine acts of creation must be allowed to reemerge.

"Feminine acts of creation?"

Yes, hijo, this is very important for you to learn. Masculine and feminine acts of creation are complementary but different. Men will typically either fight or retreat when under stress, while women will usually communicate or nurture. Men generally define themselves by their work, and they form hierarchies based on dominance. Women tend to bond together, talk about problems, care for the children. The maternal aspects of creation are what is needed now in order to heal your Mother and stop your wars. Women with maternal instincts must be given equal voice in your patriarchal governments and religions. This is the only cure in healing your Mother and your people.

In the majority of the world, women are still considered to be property, much like dogs. In many parts of the world, women and children are still being sold as slaves. But your people have made great strides in awakening to this; it is happening very rapidly and will continue to accelerate. You must help this acceleration, hijo. You must help this acceleration before it's too late.

"I'm not sure I understand what you mean by acceleration, Grandmother."

Hijo, for many hundreds of years, especially since the arrival of the religions of Abraham and the written WORD of God, your men have dominated your women. But just in a few decades, this has begun to change and continues to gain momentum. First your women were given their right to vote and own property, then women began to band together to further regain equality; now is the time to empower the maternal instincts of women to help negotiate peace for your world. You must allow this flow of energy that recognizes the feminine to keep accelerating.

"What else can you teach me about the maternal instincts of women?"

Maternal instinct is the power of Motherhood. Motherhood is about nurturing life. Good mothers care for the needs of the children, they handle their resources wisely, they communicate to resolve conflicts, they listen, they are compassionate. These are the traits that are needed now in these times of crisis and transformation. When dominant men, alpha males, meet to resolve conflict, they fail to achieve peace because peace is not in their nature. They are unable to compromise because that means they must submit to another's ideals. This situation should be crystal clear to you by now. Look around at what is happening in your world! Men will continue to challenge and fight for dominance of their ideals. That is what alpha males do. They must not be allowed to remain in control. The nurturing and communicating instincts of women are needed to negotiate peace in the world and also peace between human beings and their Mother.

"So, Grandmother, you are saying that patriarchy is a core problem in these times of crisis?"

Absolutely. Patriarchal governments and religions have demonstrated, generation after generation, that they are about power and control, which leads to aggression and war. Feminine energy has the power to dilute male aggression. It is an antidote for war. It is the antidote for the raping of your Mother. Not all men are without compassion or maternal-type instincts, and not all women have the maternal instincts combined with intellect and knowledge in adequate doses to be leaders in the transformation of consciousness. But in general, the feminine energy of women must be used to counteract the aggression of men that is the cause of war and the destruction of your Mother. Compassion must be used in decision making. Religion and nation-

alism must not be used to justify war. Production of goods must not be used as a measure of success. These are all male traits that are at the core of your crises.

"What can I do, Grandmother?"

Hijo, you work with hundreds of women every year, and through your books you touch thousands more. Share my message with women and men alike. Encourage women to form groups where they can sit in circle and discuss what must be done. Help them awaken to their Luminous Self, share with them shamanic practices so that I may speak to them directly. Support women that are fully awake so that they may learn and share aspects of spirituality where masculine and feminine energies are in balance. Provide help for grandmothers to take the place of alpha males in government. These are all things that you can do, hijo, that everyone can do and will want to do once they awaken. It is not too late. But you must begin right now!

Earth Changes

"Grandmother, many people are now looking at ancient prophecies and talking about the year 2012 as being the end of the world as we know it. Some say there is nothing we can do—that there will be a catastrophic pole shift, earthquake, volcanic eruption, or even a meteor impact that will cause mass extinction. Others are saying that 2012 represents the point of no return—that by 2012, human-made environmental catastrophes, such as global warming and deforestation, will be irreversible if we don't make major lifestyle changes right now. What can you tell me about this?"

I can tell you, hijo, that whether there is a natural catastrophe or not, there is nothing that you can do about it—so there is no point in worrying about it. If an asteroid comes or volcano erupts, you have not the power to stop it. What you do have the power to do is stop the radical changes to your Mother that humans are creating, because right now that is the biggest threat to your survival. Listen closely. You cannot continue to cut down the forests, pollute the water, and burn the flesh (coal) and blood (oil) of your Mother. Human beings are growing in number more rapidly than they know how to survive. All around your world, children are dying every day from starvation and poisoned water, but many millions more survive into a life of constant suffering. I have been watching, hijo. Every week you add more than a million people to your world. This is your biggest problem right now.

"I'm not sure what I can do to help."

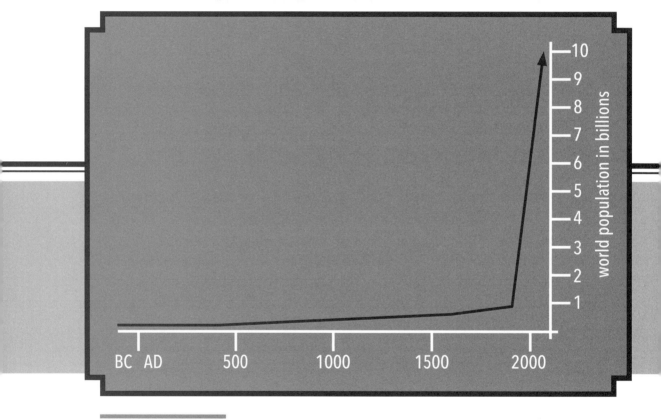

World population chart.

Then I will say it again, hijo. Empower the women! Right now, in the parts of the world where population is growing fastest, the women have little choice as to what happens inside their womb. They are dominated by men. They must be given back the power of their womb. They must be educated and given a choice about how many children to have. No mother wants to see her child suffer and die. They must be educated and, until the situation changes so that they can make their own informed decisions, they must be provided with the opportunity for contraception. Every compassionate means to control human population must be employed right away. There must be a plan for how to feed the children. It is pure common sense that this plan include how many children CAN be fed. This is huge task but one that can be handled by the women of your world if they are given the chance and the power. Look at your women, hijo. They are educated, they have the power to choose and to plan a family. Because of this, the number of new souls being born in your country is actually decreasing. This power must be spread throughout the world: the power of women to choose.

"I understand, Grandmother."

That's good. Now do something about it. While you're at it, you had better also think about another big problem that is in the realm of feminine energy: water.

Hijo, do you have any idea how many people are dying right now because they don't have clean water to drink?

Who polluted the water? Your Mother didn't do it. I didn't do it. People did it. People continue to do it, and every day it gets worse. Who has clean water to drink? That is a very important question and one that will become even more critical for everyone in the near future. There will be big trouble if alpha males are allowed to claim ownership of the water, for they will not share fairly. Women must be in charge of cleaning up the water, protecting it, and distributing it fairly.

"Are you saying that women should be in charge of the water because water is a feminine energy?"

Yes, hijo, that is part of it. Obviously there must be balance, and that is what people are missing right now. Human beings must make a plan for how they are going to save themselves or else they will just be swept away. Men are good with fire, with energies of production. They must learn to use energy in ways that do not harm your Mother. This includes putting out the fires they have already created. There is absolutely no reason that oil should be above the ground.

These fires must be put out. Men must concentrate their power away from fighting and building weapons and toward ways of putting out the fires and cleaning up the air. If I would speak plainly: men take responsibility for fire and air, women for water and soil. This is a general but effective place to start.

"It will be difficult to convince people of that, Grandmother."

Yes, I know, hijo, but there are some things on your side that you have little knowledge of—great things that can help. But sleeping people will not hear until they awaken.

Two Great Hopes

"Grandmother, please tell me more about these things on our side and how they can help."

Hijo, the biggest problem on your world right now is communication. Alpha males cannot communicate with each other, so they fight. Hypnotized people only listen to other hypnotized people because agreement feels good and feeds them what they need to hear. The greedy power brokers of your world don't listen to the poor and suffering because they lack compassion and therefore see it as a waste of time. And out of the more than 6 billion people on your world, no more than a handful are listening to the Kakaiyeri.

The good news is that there are many things you can do to overcome these obstacles. But right now when you look at them, the obstacles seem insurmountable. So I'm going to tell you something that will give you hope: when people awaken and work together, they are able to create a conscious field many times greater than any individual could. This large field of consciousness can cause a rift in the hypnotic trance of those that are asleep, so that the whisperings for them to awaken come in the form of non-ordinary feelings, thoughts, and vibrations being sent from awakened groups working together. And, hijo, when these groups learn to touch the Kakaiyeri and allow their consciousness to join in, the scales will be tipped and the Luminous Self will emerge on a global level.

"Are you saying that groups of awakened people can psychically affect those that are asleep?"

Yes, hijo. You must understand that you know very little. There is much more to your world and the omniverse than simply mind and matter. Your scientists are now beginning to get it, but you don't need science to prove it. Consciousness is underlying everything. You have already experienced that many times. As you know, sometimes this happens randomly, like when you have an idea for a new book or new invention and then you find out that the exact idea you had has just been created by someone else. The seed for that idea was planted in consciousness and randomly distributed to those open to receiving it. But this can also be cultivated intentionally. When a group of people plant a seed into consciousness, they touch the fields of other groups that carry the same seed, whether they know the other groups exist or not. It doesn't matter. A conscious network is then created between those working in the same field. In this way, even a small group, say in Somalia, can tap into the grid and connect with the energy of a much larger group in New Jersey. They may or may not be conscious of the connection, but it doesn't matter. Groups of people working on projects in the same field of consciousness help that consciousness to spread and grow even toward people who aren't part of the group. And listen to this: it is also possible and highly effective to connect with similar consciousness and behavior of people in the past. The fields of consciousness created by your forbears has not disappeared. They are still part of the great web.

"That's amazing. But could you please give me an example of this?"

If you think about the question, hijo, you will realize that you have already experienced this.

I thought about this for a while and then I remembered more than a few times that I did experience this. "Yes, Grandmother, I remember now."

Go ahead and share, hijo.

"Well, once I was on a vision quest in the Sangre de Cristo Mountains of Colorado. I had been fasting for three days. On the morning of the fourth day, I woke before dawn, and since I only allowed myself one thin blanket, I was so cold and shivering that I was ready to give up my quest. Then, as I stood waiting, the first ray of light came up over the mountain. It pierced my heart like an arrow. In that moment, I realized why ancient people worshipped the sun. I began to spontaneously sing a song of thanks to the sun that I had never heard before and move my body so as to collect energy from the sun in ways I never knew how. A few years later, I discovered an indigenous tribe with strikingly similar words to the song I had sung, and another tribe that incorporated the same style of body movements that I spontaneously made that morning."

Yes. In that moment when the sun touched you so deeply, you joined with many others before that held the exact form of reverence and gratitude for the sun as you did. Since your Luminous field was so open, instead of receiving merely whispers from that field of consciousness, you received real words and body movements.

Now, hijo, I know that the moment you just described changed your life. It was one more awakening toward your Luminous Self. Respect and gratitude for the power of Father Sun is a human act of creation that is in alignment with your Mother. But I also want you to see the bigger picture, to understand how important the great field of consciousness is and was to human civilization.

It is no mere coincidence that human crafts such as pottery, building design, and the making of tools and instruments of sound developed in much the same way throughout the world in cultures that lived far apart from each other, had no physical contact with each other, and in many cases did not even live in the same time period. This has to do with the underlying fabric of consciousness shared by all. Do you see the implications for this? Do you see how this is affecting your culture?

"Wow! If I understand what you're saying, this means that in a similar way as ancient people throughout the world shared a consciousness on how to make tools and pottery, the same could be done now with the sharing of the need to awaken to the Luminous Self."

That's right, hijo. Instead of your culture sharing the idea that shiny new things are better than old things that still serve well, or that money is the key to the good life, a critical mass of people could whisper the truth into the consciousness of the hypnotized. But listen, now that you understand this, you can take it even further. Most of the ancient cultures we spoke of did not intentionally share their conscious knowledge of tools or pottery design with other cultures. They didn't even know they existed. But the awakened ones in your culture now have the ability to intentionally use this knowledge to help save the world. The more individuals and groups that project similar energy patterns and thought waves, the easier it is for others to receive the messages and join in. This is the great hope for humankind, as it is the ultimate form of communication. But, hijo, that is not all. I have more to share with you about this. Are you still with me?

"Yes, Grandmother, you are beginning to give me great hope that human consciousness can be transformed into a more healthy form during these times of great change."

Good. Now listen closely. I fear that your people are so deeply hypnotized that it will take too long to awaken them without the use of every tool you have. That is why I'm going to suggest that you use two powerful tools on opposite ends of the spectrum.

The first is your technology of global communications. This tool can help to speed up the process of awakening when it is used to draw people together from around the world with the intention of planting specific seeds of transformation in global human consciousness. Instead of one group in one place in one point in time, you now have the power to gather thousands of groups all around the world at the same time. This will amplify the message so that it is heard louder and by more people each time it is done. Do you understand?

"Yes."

The second tool is even more important, for it is little known or thought about by the hypnotized: communication with and through the Kakaiyeri.

Do you see where I'm going with this, hijo?

"Yes, I think so! I have thought about this before, but not on a global level. I think what you're saying is that in a similar way to how we humans spread messages throughout global consciousness to other humans, the spirits of nature, the Kakaiyeri, spread messages throughout the natural world. We can spread our message through them, throughout the world, if we simply communicate our messages to them."

That's right. But in a similar way to how your global Internet can form groups of people around the globe to send messages more rapidly into the consciousness of human beings, these groups can also at the same time convey messages to the Kakaiyeri so that the natural world is informed of your intentions with the same speed. This is the second great hope for humanity. You have already developed the speed of communication necessary to save the world. Now you simply have to put it to proper use.

"You give me great hope, Grandmother; please tell me more about sending messages through the Kakaiyeri."

Hijo, as you know, everything is connected. The essences and energies that manifest in your world—the spirits of rivers, lakes, forests, gardens, animals, birds, fish, insects, mountains, deserts, canyons, and all the other forms of life—share in a mutually informative body, the body of your Mother. When you help a forest, you help the sky; when you plant a garden, you help a forest; when you help the ocean, you help the rain; when you help the rain, you help the forest. You see, hijo, it's all the same body. So in any place that you are, when you send a message to the spirits of nature that live there, your message will be spread throughout the whole web of life. Like dropping a pebble into a pond, the effects of the pebble will be seen more apparently in the close area where it was dropped in the water—but the whole body of water feels the pebble. What I am suggesting you do is use your ability to communicate with others around the world to drop millions of pebbles of intention into the great sea of consciousness.

"Grandmother, many people have no experience in working with the Kakaiyeri; how do you suggest we proceed in delivering our messages of intention?"

It is all about demonstrating reciprocity, compassion, unconditional love, and respect for the essences and energies that sustain life on your world. The ultimate expression would be for an immediate and complete reversal of the industrial attack upon your Mother. But we know that won't happen right away—there are still too many hypnotized alpha males that think they are in charge of your world.

So gather awakened people from around the world, form circles where people can gather, give thanks, make offerings. Build shrines, altars, and temples that do not keep nature out but rather invite the spirits in. Speak to the spirits of your place, work tirelessly to heal your local, natural area. Plant gardens. Even if you live in the city, plant on a balcony or at a friend's house. Hijo, every single action, no matter how big or how small, will be felt and spread throughout the web of life.

"On the other side of the spectrum, Grandmother, what about those who have awakened and have already been working to heal the natural world and reclaim reciprocity? What is the next step for us?"

This will all depend on the person. You must ask the Kakaiyeri for your personal tasks. Depending on how open you are to hear the truth, you will receive your answer. For example, you, hijo; many years ago, you asked your question in the sacred desert of the Wirrarika and received your answer—to write your first book, to help people connect with the Kakaiyeri. You were awake enough to hear that truth, but not awake enough to fully accept it. You were not a writer. So even though the message to write a book came to you crystal clear, your mind was confused. It took you more than two years to fully accept your task and another year to complete it. Much of that time was spent simply arranging your life so you had "time" to write. You had to make sacrifices, change your attitude toward certain things, and arrange your life so that you could complete your task. This will be the same for everyone around you. Everyone that hears the voice of the Kakaiyeri will have to change, for change is the only thing that will help you.

The tasks that people receive may come as a surprise and may not be readily accepted. You may be asked to change your career to work closer to the acts of creation of your Mother. You may be asked to take the next step toward sustainability and move to a community that lives off the grid. You may be asked to help the starving and dying children in other parts of the world. You may be asked to be the one in your area that forms a group of conscious intenders to plant seeds of change into human consciousness. You may be asked to do many of these things and many more. It is all up to the individual and the level of truth about their current life that they are ready to accept and the amount of change they are willing to make.

"Grandmother, why is it the tasks we are given by the Kakaiyeri are often so different than what we expect and so difficult to accomplish?"

The tasks you are given have nothing to do with who you think you are and everything to do with who you really are. When your Mother gave you the task to write your first book, she could clearly see that your task should be to share in that way, and that the process would also bring you closer to your Luminous Self. For you it seemed strange. It is normal to ask, "Why am I given this task I know nothing about, wouldn't it be better if I use my knowledge to contribute something closer to a field in which I already have skills?"

You see, hijo, sometimes you will be asked to contribute your knowledge about what you already know. Sometimes you will be asked to do something completely new. This is because many times people think they know everything about a certain field, so they are less open to discovering something new. Many times the greatest discoveries are made by "accident." The most important thing to remember here is that you cannot keep going down the road you are on. Your people must change. They must change their minds, their hearts, their lifestyles, and many of their jobs, habits, goals, and expectations of life.

When your time has come to receive a task directly from the spirits, the best thing you can do for yourself and the world is to go for it, no matter how strange or difficult it may seem. Follow your heart and live in the Luminous Self, and everything else will take care of itself.

"Grandmother, you know that I have been through this many times, that I have been given various tasks throughout the years that have tested me in ways I never would have believed possible. I have had many successes and worked through a lot of failures. I would like to hear any advice you give for when we hit that place of giving up—when the task and the challenges surrounding us seem too big to overcome."

The Power of Ritual

Hijo, you have felt the power of being in the flow of creation—those times when your actions were being supported by the power of creation, so that when a specific person was needed, they would show up; when a certain set of circumstances was necessary for a project to go on, the pieces seemed to magically fall into place. In those moments, your Luminous Self was guiding your actions to consciously co-create with your Mother. Your actions were involved in something much bigger than the purely human sphere, where most human actions are centered.

Now, you have also experienced what it feels like when you are not in the flow, when you have wandered off your path. In those times, things do not flow easily. Little problems always seem to creep up, which eventually turn into bigger obstacles and then, eventually, failure.

What has repeatedly brought you back on to the path is your reawakening to your Luminous Self. You could say that in those times when you strayed from your path you had fallen back asleep. But you had the tools of consciousness to reawaken from your nap. Over the years, you have been conditioned and trained in the ways of the Luminous Self. You have learned ancient rituals of conscious connection and co-creation with your Mother, and you have been taught the ways of the shaman directly from the Kakaiyeri and your Grandfather. This is what you lean on when you come up against your obstacles. Like a river, you flow around or over them, sometimes even using your power to move them out of the way. Your consciousness is like the water, and it gains momentum when your actions are in line with creation.

"But Grandmother, please explain to me how all of the actions of human beings that flow against creation are so successful. Taking more oil and coal and trees from our Mother faster than they can be created goes against creation. I don't understand how people have been so successful at creating these industries when they so clearly flow contrary to natural creation."

You are thinking too small, hijo. Your question has to do with the evolution of human consciousness. Up until this point, your people have learned to survive, be comfortable, and proliferate through using the energies of the Kakaiyeri without giving anything back. But now you are waking up to the fact that you can't continue to do that. Your president and the rest of the asleep alpha males that advise him are doing a terrific job helping people awaken. How? Because as people start to rise from their slumber, it becomes more and more clear to them that the actions of your government leaders are completely the opposite of what is needed. As this happens, people become disillusioned and then frustrated and finally awaken to the truth. So you see, hijo, for humans to join in conscious co-creation with their Mother, they first have to experience unconscious co-creation. Your species is evolving past the need for unbridled power at any cost and into the use of power in re-joining with creation. You needed to take the need for power to the extreme before you could see the need to slow down before you crash. That is what is happening right now. But if you don't put on the brakes right now, it will be too late, and your people will crash right into the wall of suffering.

"To be able to put on the breaks in a large enough way, many more people will need to become awake."

Yes, hijo. Your people need to change their perception of the world. At first, the perception was mind over matter, then mind over energy, for all matter is energy. Now you are being asked to meld mind and energy in a conscious manner. Many of the ways of doing this are what you call shamanic practices. Shamanic healers work with energy. Shamanics is physics. You are working with energies, and right now your task is to amplify the consciousness of the Luminous Self so that enough people awaken to save your world.

"Could you explain amplifying consciousness?"

You amplify consciousness when you make rituals and offerings, hijo. Through your offerings and rituals, you're intensifying your intentions and enlarging the energy field. It's like when you offer food to your Grandfather Fire. You give fuel to his energy and he grows stronger and more intense. The same goes for consciousness. The fuel is intention that is concentrated and intensified by energetic rituals and offerings. When the fuel is intensified, perception and consciousness expand and enlarge.

You have learned very powerful forms of offering from your Wirrarika brothers and sisters. They have not forgotten the face of their Mother and understand the need for energetic reciprocity. But now, hijo, you are being asked to bring that knowledge to your people in a context that is meaningful to their lives.

"For many years I have been sharing that knowledge, Grandmother. I don't know what else to do. I have tried to share with people that offerings and rituals must be meaningful to our everyday lives or they are useless. To steadfastly hold on to outdated practices is foolish; to copy the practices of others is even worse. We need to continually modify our practices to keep time with the way we live now."

You have the basic understanding of this, hijo, so now you simply need to learn more, go deeper. Share with the people what you have learned about the power of ritual and offerings while you yourself go even deeper into amplifying consciousness.

Part Three:
Practical Applications of the
First Shamans' Teachings

Chapter 6

Using Altars to Alter and Amplify Consciousness

Grandmother Growth has made it abundantly clear that we have the power to alter human consciousness on a grand scale by amplifying our intent through the use of rituals and offerings. But let us not forget that the rituals of our current state of transformation, and the churches, temples, and altars where they are carried out, are not the ends but the means of discovering and honoring the altar of our soul as being one with creation. Every human being can be a shrine of love, an altar of hope. The altars of our time need not promote the validity of one religion or faith over another, but rather unite all faiths into actions leading to peace between all people, people with the tangible face of spirit: our Mother Earth.

It is time that we view our sacred places, such as churches, temples, altars, etc., not as places that segregate the sacred and the mundane or differentiate between the holy and the unholy but rather as places and spaces where we go to honor the interconnection of all life and spirit.

This altar of center uses three levels of offerings, hung by saplings that lend their support to this transitory spiritual portal. (Photo: James Endredy)

The altars, and the ways of creating and working with them, that I offer in this chapter serve to function as places where one can leave the fast-paced modern world for a while to discover and honor one's unity with the divine. In this way, the altar becomes a sanctuary not because it separates us but because it serves as a tool of transformation toward uniting us with the divine, which is everything. If the goal is to live in harmony with creation, we first must awaken to our Luminous Self. Altars, rituals, and offerings made in harmony with creation then become the tools of our awakening.

The Altar of Center

To begin the practical aspects of the First Shamans' teachings, the concepts and rituals pertaining to altars, shrines, and offerings stand significantly in the forefront of actions that align us with creation and aid in the transformation of consciousness toward conscious co-creation. The ritual use of the altar as a way of creating a portal into the consciousness of the center of creation is a key action employed by ancient shamans, priests, and priestesses as well as modern mystics and healers. The use of altars in this sense reunites the human world with the source of life and creation. The sacred and universal space created by such altars allows us to move past our human-centered version of reality by expanding our awareness and consciousness to include the more-than-human worlds of nature and spirit, to which we are ever connected.

One of the most powerful altar configurations that I have experienced is designed specifically to unite us with that which lies at the center of creation and that has been referred to by humanity as the Great Spirit, Unkulukulu, Atman, Wakan-Tanka, Yahweh, Allah, Jah, Ngai, Brahman, Itzamna, and Universal Life Force, among countless others. While it is not my intention to lead this into a discussion of the similarities or differences between the usage of these names, or even into a discussion with regards to monotheism, polytheism, pantheism, paganism, and many other -isms, I do greatly respect the power of intentionally opening and awakening to the powerful, mystical, and numinous process of creation, especially when this leads us to be touched with the qualities of awe and humility that lead to states of peacefulness and harmony.

Therefore, this first type of altar I'm going to share, as well as the many others following it, is designed not to support or deny any specific religion but rather to connect us in a pure and direct way to a portal that lies at the beginning of a new path of awareness and understanding of our role as human beings and how we might fit into the grander scheme of creation.

This altar of center is specifically designed to be a portal where one may touch that which lies at the center of creation. This center might be called "energy" in the modern world, the ancient Maya called it Itz, my Wirrarika mentors call it Kupuri. What I am referring to is that which gives power to the blood or milk of humans and animals, the light and heat of the sun, an egg, the bud of a flower, the nourishment of water.

For time immemorial, shamans, mystics, and holy people of all persuasions have journeyed to the place where time, matter, and consciousness meet, the place that emanates the sacred life force. This place—called Xibalba, "the place of awe," by the ancient Maya—is a real place if for no other reason than millions of people throughout time have traveled there and in doing so have made it real.

The altar of center is the place created by the power of our intention, where we can travel to Xibalba to reunite with the sacred life-force, respectfully honor the energy of creation, and realign ourselves in such a way as to awaken to a life of peace and harmony.

altar construction

This altar is constructed in the open air, for its design is all about connecting us to that which is all around us, which is much different than churches and temples that inherently keep nature "outside." The foundation for the altar is four trees, usually saplings that are growing from the earth close enough to place a small platform in between them. A platform is tied to the trees at the corners, thus connecting it to the four cardinal directions. This platform, normally of wood, symbolizes the "middle world," which is the physical reality we know of and where we live our daily lives. The ground beneath the platform altar is the "underworld," where the roots of trees and plants, and the billions of organisms that give life to the soil, reside. This is a place of life that we normally don't see, but it is just as valid and important as the life aboveground that we are accustomed to. The space above the altar is the "upper world" that joins our little blue-green planet, our Mother Earth, to the whirling precession of satellites around our sun, and our solar system with the greater galaxy.

In the center of the altar, above the platform, is a raised (or hanging) area for a basket, or hollowed and halved gourds, or chalices, that symbolize the "hole," "opening," or "portal" from which we can travel through and where the vital life-force of Xibalba pours in. This raised center area completes the ancient symbolism of the world tree, or axis mundi, found in so many spiritual traditions throughout the globe. For this reason, the altar of center can also be thought of as the altar of galactic center, for in its symbolic construction we intentionally acknowledge the link between our planet and the center of the galaxy. In this time of great transformation on our planet, it is more than interesting to note that modern astronomers have recently discovered residing in the center of our galaxy a giant black hole. And many researchers and scientists are now saying that our solar system is, or soon will be, passing through a rare alignment with the center of the galaxy.[11]

altar preparation

Above any other consideration, it is the power of intention that activates any altar. Even if you had absolutely nothing to place on the altar, or physically offer, your power of intention would still be the force that opens the door to Xibalba. But if we do have them available, there are many essences and energies that can aid us in focusing the power of our intention and assist us in our tasks. The manner in which you activate and use your altar is strictly personal, but as always I suggest that we take clues from the ancestors and then add those items and procedures that make sense to our current ways of life.

In this way, the first step in preparation is to "feed" the altar with energy and actions of reciprocity. Since the altar has three main levels, all three must be fed. Below are suggestions for all three levels:

THE UNDERWORLD: Under the platform, either sitting on the ground and/or buried in the ground, we acknowledge the normally unseen forces beneath us that give us life.

- Roots from your garden that are placed on the ground of the altar signify your awareness of the complex web of life and how the roots of the underground world produce the living world above.

---

11 For more on this subject, see works by John Major Jenkins.

- Soil from your garden or a sacred place. This living soil can be placed on a "bed," which could be a small tray, plate, or open box, that, when placed in the altar, acknowledges your understanding and gratitude that our Mother Earth is alive, and that our physical body is an extension of her body.
- Any uncooked (raw) food items represent your thanks for the bounty we receive from the energy of the underworld.
- A cup or bowl of virgin (spring) water (the fresher the better).
- You can place special stones, or tékas, on the ground, especially at the corners at the base of the four trees but I usually prefer to sit my tékas on the platform, since they are now my companions in the middle world.

THE MIDDLE WORLD: On the platform, we ritually acknowledge the gifts of our physical reality and demonstrate our current place in the world.

- Cooked food items such as bread and stews can be placed on the altar platform to represent our human interaction with the world and can then be blessed during the activation of the altar and eaten afterwards.
- Thanks and acknowledgment can be given by placing actual items or representations of important tools that you use, photos or effigies of special people, or anything that helps you or gives meaning to your life.
- Tékas, flowers, feathers, or whatever else that helps you or brings a sense of beauty to your life and altar.
- Items that represent to you changes that you would like to make in your life or see happen in the world. We can create positive energy at this level by acknowledging things like war, oppression, extraction of fossil fuels, deforestation, etc., and during the ceremony making prayers for the resolution of these situations.

THE UPPER WORLD: The center basket (or other types of containers that are placed in the upper region) represents the sacred life-force of creation and also connection to the numinous aspects of life.

- Juice, milk, water, sap, blood, infused oils—all represent the lifeblood of creation. Once the portal to Xibalba is opened and during the latter stages of the ceremony, these fluids can be used to bless other items in the altar with the energy of creation flowing from Xibalba.

- Sacred items or tools that you use to specifically connect with the numinous aspects of life or that you use in healing work or other spiritual ceremonies.

altar activation

Now that we are ready to actively work with the altar we have created, it is important to be absolutely clear about why we are doing it. I know of many people who have used the force of intention and the power of ritual to open portals to other worlds but then connected with powers that were actually harmful to them. And of course throughout history there have been those types of shamans and priests who have intentionally called upon the forces I refer to as anti-creation to promote sickness and death for the misguided elevation of their own power. We must acknowledge that acts of anti-creation not only exist, but they are very powerful. The destructive energy that leads men to take oil and coal faster than it can be created, that imbues a false sense of power and security in those responsible for waging wars and killing millions of innocent human and other beings, is just as real as the energy that promotes peace and balance. In activating your altar, you will feel power. It is vitally important to stay focused on channeling that power toward actions of conscious co-creation and not allowing the rush of energy coming in to persuade or seduce you into harnessing it for selfish reasons. For this reason, I suggest that you now perform a formal ritual of intention.

This is simply to get the energy moving and flowing in the direction that you want. I suggest that you use your voice and express through words your intentions out loud to the items on the altar, your human and nonhuman companions around you, and all the beings both seen and unseen around your altar. If necessary, you can even do this while purifying the area with smoke from a meaningful source. Historically, the use of fragrant incense, bundles of sage or sweet grass, or pieces of dried cedar or copal resin, have been used for this, and they can help you switch out of your ordinary thought processes to be ready to experience the mysteries you are entering into.

Once your intentions have been clearly stated, the altar can be safely activated by a combination of movement, sonic vibration, and intention. Movement is normally initiated by walking in slow circles around the altar so as to join with the circular (or, more properly, elliptical) movement of our Mother Earth. As the activation proceeds, the walk can be alternately sped up or slowed down, or turned into a dance either fast or slow.

Sonic vibrations are created by using instruments of sound such as the drum, rattle, guitar, violin, or any other kind of device, as well as most importantly your own voice in the form of talking, chanting, and singing.

Intention for opening the portal to the "source" or "center" is accomplished by expressing your desires, prayers, and offerings through your words, songs, and movements. Begin by making this a natural extension of your original statement of intent, and then allow it to enlarge by letting your Luminous Self take charge and your ego sit and watch silently. Some suggestions here include:

FOUNDATIONAL PHASE

- Express the reasons for the items you included in the altar, one by one, from bottom to top. Don't rush this procedure. At the deepest levels, the essences and energies will eventually sing "through" you. You can do this as many times as necessary until you feel a shift in consciousness happening.

- Experiment with the effects of raising and lowering the octave of your voice as you express to the altar. I have found that most shamans raise the pitch of their voice in certain moments, as this tends to aid power and imbue a certain quality of sacredness.

GENERATING MOMENTUM PHASE

- Open a portal to your sacred sites and other places that have touched you, and relive special moments of connection. Feel the special qualities of the place; see yourself as "watching a movie" of you being there and also see out of your eyes as you did when you were there, and try to experience as much of your other senses as well.

- Recollect the essences and energies of the wind, water, soil, and fire by reliving special moments when they touched you. Feel again your feet in the ocean, the wind blowing your hair, the heat and light of the fire and sun, and the sand, soil, and grass between your toes.

ACKNOWLEDGMENTS AND PRAYERS FOR THE WORLD PHASE

- Express your personal intentions of aligning with co-creation.

- Send out your prayers to our Mother Earth for the awakening of humanity so that the raping of her body will end.

- Send out your prayers, one by one, to the individual spirits of the animals, birds, sea inhabitants, trees, and plants. Call to them by name, and express your desire to be in alignment and balance with them.

- Make prayers for the hungry and oppressed people of our world, and express intentions for aid.

- Acknowledge both the soldiers and the innocents that are dying right now from misguided concepts of power, and offer prayers of peace.

- Pray for the awakening of our world leaders, that they may shed the need for dominating others who don't share their same ideals.

- Express intentions to help in the education of people in countries where human procreation is out of control to the point of major suffering.

PORTAL PHASE

- While still moving around the altar and allowing sonic vibrations and the power of intention to shift your consciousness, begin to go to the next level by uniting even further with the structure and symbolism of the altar and traveling up the central axis of the world tree.

- Embody *In Lak'ech* (see practice on page 158). You are everything, and everything is you. Mind and matter are ripples in the same pool. Allow your consciousness to touch the center of the pool and merge with creation.

Altars of Healing

A powerful healing altar is multifaceted in order to address healing at multiple levels: physical, mental, environmental, and spiritual. Oftentimes, physical maladies result from emotional crises or imbalances of a spiritual nature. Spiritual crises often result from environmental maladies or physical concerns. So in order to effect true healing, it's necessary that we address our total organism.

The physical manifestation of the healing altar will then have at least four parts, or "layers." Round altars can be divided into four by placing a cross in the middle. This gesture and the symbolism it reflects immediately connects you with ancient healers of many traditions.

Another powerful way for the healing altar to manifest is in tiers, or floors, each representing an aspect of the human organism while also acknowledging the different "worlds" we live in simultaneously.

In both of the constructions I have mentioned, the idea is the same: to physically represent actions at multiple levels of healing and concentrate your intention by using the altar to aid you in the manifestation of healing. For example, if I am to facilitate healing from a personal relationship that has ended and left me feeling hurt, I must recognize that my feelings are my own responsibility, not theirs. In this case, at the emotional or mental level I need to understand that ill feelings toward this person don't do anyone any good, so to facilitate healing I need to wish this person good intentions for the future and that they will learn and grow from the experience, just as I will. Items that give rise to an emotional or even intellectual recognition of this would be appropriate to place in the mental quadrant of the round altar or mental level of a tiered altar. Since our human relationships are so complex, these items can vary greatly, depending on the circumstance. It might be that you place an item in this level that symbolizes an important goal or project to this person. In this way, you are facilitating healing through reversing any negative feelings toward the person by intentionally wishing them well.

On a physical level, in this example there will be a physical absence of the person in your life that you will have to deal with. You may ask yourself how you will spend the time you normally spent with them, or how you will accomplish the physical tasks that they shared in your life. For this level, you would place items that symbolize the actions at a physical level that you will make part of your healing. "Replacing" time spent with them could be helped by reconnecting with old friends, starting new projects, spending time on things you haven't done in a while, etc. There are always solutions to situations that seem like a "problem" on a physical level if you tackle the situation from a positive point of view.

Environmentally, this example will require you to clear the space that you shared with this person. This can be done in myriad ways, such as removing personal items left behind, physically cleaning the places you shared, rearranging furniture, and performing rituals of cleansing by burning some sage or cedar in the space to release the cleansing smoke of these special companions of ours. Items for your altar will then include representations of these types of actions.

On a spiritual level, you are acknowledging that no matter how painful a situation, there is always the opportunity for growth and further awakening to the mysteries of life. Oftentimes the hardest lessons are the ones that spur us to then soar to greater heights of compassion, joy, and awareness. Your altar of healing is the perfect place to help manifest your movement to higher levels of spiritual awareness by the experiences and lessons you learned through your past relationship with this person. Use your altar to express and be thankful for what you have gained by sharing time with this person.

Obviously, emotional healing from an ended relationship is one of thousands of situations of healing. But in all cases, if we work from the four basic realities of consciousness we have a better chance of facilitating true healing. When dealing with physical healing from illness or injury, altars can be used effectively in hospitals or other types of care facilities. By inviting visitors and loved ones to participate in the altar (especially children), the level of healing energy generated by the altar will be raised significantly. The power of human intention is a measurable force that even science now recognizes. Altars of healing have the power to transform at all levels of creation when used with intention, creativity, and connection.

An important consideration with healing altars is that they are constructed to be temporary. They are created to facilitate healing you or someone else and therefore are used to help us pass through something and accomplish a specific outcome. Creating them with this intention will help to generate their healing function, and when they have run their course they should be dismantled with thoughtfulness and respect.

My manifestation altar for this book. (Photo: Nancy Bartell)

Altars of Manifestation and Creation

We are all imbued with a unique blend of creative abilities that make us who we are as individuals, while at the same time we all share in the collective processes of creation. Clarifying our specific tasks in life is the first step toward using our specific talents in aligning with creation. Many of the techniques and tools outlined in this section can help us to realize what we are being asked to do with our life, and once we realize these tasks, altars of manifestation can help us to focus our energy and intent on accomplishing our goals.

For example, about six months ago it became very clear to me that one of my tasks was to write this book. I have a couple of rituals that I have used in the past to help me with writing, and I used these from the start of this project. However, during the writing, many things happened in my life that I couldn't ignore. The emotional departure of a loved one from my home, the birth of a niece, the entrance of a special woman in my life, roof leaks in the ceiling of my house, the installation of a new woodstove, etc. are all situations that have taken me away from my writing. So facing a deadline to my publisher, I found it helpful to create a new altar of manifestation to help focus my intention on completing my goal. This altar includes the careful positioning of my previous books as a tangible reminder that I am capable of creating this current book. It also contains representations of the First Shamans, including a sacred gourd of soil and rock, a special candle and pieces of resinous wood that I use to bring forth Grandfather Fire, some of my tékas, and sacred objects from previous altars, among other things.

By having this altar in a prominent location in my house and in full view from the area where I write, it has served to inspire me and remind me of my task in many moments when I could be easily distracted. It is this type of helpful energy that an altar of manifestation can serve to create.

These types of altars can serve to help manifest a specific task, such as the above example, or they can help generate creativity in general in your life. Maybe you don't have a specific task on your plate or in your mind right now, or maybe you have just completed a task and are now taking time to recharge or get clear on your next goal. In this case, an altar of creativity can help you to open up to your creative talents. You can create it by simply allowing yourself to express your creativity and self-expression in any way that you are inspired to do so.

Rahelio with medicine wheel in Sedona, Arizona. Rahelio is a healer, guide, and astrologer in Sedona who has been working most of his life in the construction and ceremonial use of medicine wheels. (Photo: Rahelio Rodriguez)

Altars of Transformation

It used to be that for many people, one occupation or life circumstance occupied a domi-nant portion of a their life. You learned to be a blacksmith, a carpenter, or a homemaker, and you spent the better portion of your life engaged in that activity or in the same so-cial class, educational bracket, etc. But in these times of rapid change, this is no longer the norm. It is very common to change occupations, partners, income levels, and even spiritual affiliations sometimes many times during a lifetime. For this reason, at many levels, we are now commonly experiencing moments of rapid personal transformation.

Transitioning in a healthy way through these transformations can be aided by altars that recognize and honor the various stages of our life. Typically we are accustomed to recognizing and sanctifying the marriage between two people with the use of a sacred altar. This type of spiritual energy, this feeling of sacredness that employs the altar in helping us to place our actions and intentions in front of God, Goddess, Creator, can be invoked to mark many other types of major transformations and transitions in our lives.

Life-changing events that can be made even more special and sacred by the creation of a transformational-type altar include the birth of a child, changing of occupation, starting school, moving your residence, beginning a new spiritual stage, awakening to a new task in your life, and passing through a formal initiation that marks a significant passage from one stage of life to the next—for example, from child to adult or from adult to elder.

Transformational altars can also be employed to add awareness and significance to our relationship with the natural world. Beginning or deepening your relationship with an animal spirit or other being, such as a plant or tree, or connecting with the energy of a sacred place or power spot[12] are all circumstances where the creation of an altar can exponentially increase the energy surrounding your new relationship.

Altars Honoring Creation

the medicine wheel

An estimated 20,000 stone circles of many different sizes and configurations existed in North America before the Europeans arrived. These "medicine wheels" have emerged again in modern times as tools that help us to understand ourselves in relation to the

---

12 See *Ecoshamanism*.

Finger labyrinth, Santa Lucca Cathedral. (Photo: Jean-Christophe Benoist)

universe and to respect ourselves and our relation to other life forms and our Mother Earth.

The medicine wheel is a symbol of the circle of life. In its various forms, the circle, or wheel, evokes an inner response as it touches our innate knowing of the power of the circle in manifesting life, death, rebirth, and both the seasons of the year and the seasons of our lives.

Traditions and techniques for the using the medicine wheel vary widely, as these stone circles are used throughout the world in hundreds of cultures. In this time of great transformation, the usage of the medicine wheel is not simply symbolic. It can be used to tangibly evoke our sacred reconnection to the numinous aspects of life and creation and to bring all people together.

In 1992, Hopi elder Thomas Banyacya addressed the United Nations and delivered the message of the necessity to live in harmony with all beings. Later, he spontaneously called on all the participants, including U.N. officials, to form a great circle. Each person silently said a prayer for peace. Forming a circle of unity comprised of people from the four corners of the earth is more than just a symbolic act; it gives us hope that in these troubled times, we can all work together for the common good.

labyrinths

The labyrinth, a single path moving through a circular form that leads to the center and then back again, is an ancient tool for altering consciousness. According to Kimberly Lowelle Saward, Ph.D., president of the Labyrinth Society, "The labyrinth is an archetype of transformation. Its transcendent nature knows no boundaries, crossing time and cultures with ease. The labyrinth serves as a bridge from the mundane to the divine."[13] As a response to the many crises of our times, labyrinths are now finding their way into many public places, churches, hospitals, and community centers.

Walking a labyrinth is a right-brain activity (creative, intuitive, imaginative) and can induce or enhance a contemplative or meditative state of mind. As the body moves, the mind quiets, allowing access to alternate forms of awareness and perception. Within the gentle meandering of the labyrinth, the release of pain and sorrow, of negative ways of

---

13 The Labyrinth Society, http://labyrinthsociety.org/

thinking, or of the difficulty in making a tough decision gives way to the loving, healing presence of the divine.

The growing popularity of labyrinths makes them relatively easy to find and use. There are also companies that specialize in labyrinth construction, and you can even purchase portable labyrinths, usually made of cloth, that can be placed on the ground. Aside from walking labyrinths, there are also "finger" labyrinths that can be used by tracing their patterns with your fingers. In the ninth century, Santa Lucca cathedral in Italy had a labyrinth on the wall for people to trace with their fingers before they entered the cathedral. This was understood to be a way of quieting the mind before entering the sacred place.

shrines

To me, a shrine is more about displaying dedication and honor, while an altar is more about action. Shrines are often built and used to honor the life and death of a person, but I have employed them in many other ways, such as the completion of a project, an anniversary, and especially when relating to the natural world and the cosmos.

I have created and helped many others create shrines for sacred places in nature, such as for mountains, lakes, and special trees that become like friends and mentors. Shrines can be powerful and effective tools for fostering humility in front of the great mystery of life we are part of.

Offerings

Offerings are a wonderful opportunity to creatively express our intentions to the spiritual essences and energies around and inside of us. Having worked ceremonially with many different spiritual traditions and faiths, I have found that offerings can be loosely grouped into categories so that we may better understand their implications and usages.

> VOTIVE OFFERINGS: This is a broad category of offerings that can be made to win the goodwill of the spirits by feeding them energy, or offered during a time of trouble or crisis, or even simply to express gratitude

and connection. To express this type of offering, historically candles have been used, as well as many other items, such as statues of wax, wood, stone, and metal; cups and chalices; swords, axes, and arrowheads; as well as feathers, pelts, and skulls. Votive offerings are the most common "everyday" type of offering that keep us connected and awake to the mystery and magic of life during the course of our day-to-day affairs.

FOOD OFFERINGS: These differ from votive offerings in the sense that they offer energetic sustenance that provides life and symbolizes the desire to nurture. From Buddhism to Santería, Egypt to the Americas, every day thousands of food offerings are made by people throughout the world.

PROPITIATORY OFFERINGS: Appeasing angry spirits from neglect, betrayal, or even attack is what these offerings aim to do. Historically, many cultures made these types of offerings, even in the form of human sacrifice, to appease the gods. But in this day and age, it might be wise for us to look at this type of offering in a different way. For example, in my work with trees and natural places of power, I have found that forests, jungles, bodies of water, and mountains—pretty much wherever the human enterprise has inflicted damage upon nature—are not exactly "happy" with us. It is an extremely positive gesture to make propitiatory offerings to the natural world as both a sign of desiring reciprocity instead of destruction and also to help heal our psychological trauma resulting from our disconnection with nature.

SUBSTITUTIONARY OFFERINGS: These offerings are meant to take the place of an endangered life. I have seen this happening more and more lately, in many diverse forms of offering. For example, when developers come with bulldozers, people are saving special trees that are sacred to them by offering to protect the trees and by negotiating with the developers to build around the trees or alter their designs to incorporate them. In this case, the risk of physical injury, time, and energy is offered as a substitution for killing. Another example is when people substitute their resources for stopping the killing of endangered species. Countless substitutionary offerings can be made that not only help save the lives of innocent beings, but in doing so connect us in the most tangible way to the interconnection of all life and, thus, our Luminous Self.

PREVENTATIVE OFFERINGS: These head off the need for substitutionary and other types of offerings to restore balance. These are precautionary-type offerings that are made with foresight and intuition. For example, you make an offering related to educating children about smoking, birth control, etc., to prevent them from making bad decisions. I prefer to call these "proactive offerings," but the word *preventative* gets the point across strongly.

INITIATORY OFFERINGS: During this time of great transformation for both our species and the planet, many people are rediscovering that sacred rites of passage and initiations that mark growth and transition during different periods of our lives are extremely important practices that we would do well to revive. Offerings made during these types of ceremonies and rituals support the initiate during the transition and on into the next phase of their life.

FOUNDATIONAL OFFERINGS: These types of offerings are often conducted in a group or family setting with the purpose of giving strength and intention when embarking on major endeavors, such as the building of a home, starting a new business, moving to a new area, etc. Offerings of this type can be extremely valuable for setting the intent of a group so that the members are energetically together in the spirit of their new project.

THANKSGIVING OFFERINGS: These important offerings complete a successful cycle or endeavor and are made in response to good fortune or successful resolution of a problem. Displaying thanks and gratitude for what you have and the things you accomplish are humble acts of creation that provide increased appreciation for life.

SANCTIFICATION AND BLESSING OFFERINGS: In this context, blessing is a form of powerful intent offered to sanctify or give special sacred significance to an item, person, or situation.

Offerings are an often misunderstood aspect of shamanism, but they are one of the most important. Sadly, they are almost nonexistent in the practices of modern people. One of the most powerful ways that we access Xibalba is by making offerings that display our unity with creation.

Chapter 7

The Day Creators

In our transformation toward being more caring and compassionate people that live in flow with creation, one of the central issues becomes how to spend our time—simply, what we do during our day. As we get away from judging the success of our day on how much we can produce and move closer to basing our day on aligning with creation, it becomes helpful to have guidance as to where to focus our energy.

The First Shamans have suggested that the Mayan sacred calendar can be useful for this purpose, and I couldn't agree more. At its core level, the Mayan sacred calendar is designed specifically to align humanity with the cycles of creation.

As with most everything these days, there is lots of controversy between scholars, independent researchers, and spiritualists about how to use the Mayan calendar. I do not wish to join in this controversy, simply because I don't believe there is one right or wrong way to view this complex topic. Even among modern Maya there are varying uses and interpretations for the calendar. For example, in Mayan culture the shaman/priests who work very closely with the calendar are called "Day Keepers." But when asking Day Keepers from different Mayan villages a simple question, like "What is the first day of the calendar?" you will receive many different answers. Although academic scholars give various explanations for this, I, and many others who have worked with the calendar in a "spiritual" context, believe that since the sacred calendar runs in a sequence of continuous cycles (unlike our Gregorian calendar, which seemingly runs in a straight line, starting with "The Year of Our Lord AD 1"), there is simply no reason to agree on when it starts. The Mayan sacred calendar of creation is like a wheel spinning through time.

Now, unlike us, the Maya actually had more than one calendar. In most cases, they actually used at least two calendars to describe each day. One was a civil, or "business," calendar based on solar revolution of 365 days, much like our Gregorian calendar. But the other was a sacred, or "divinatory," calendar based on twenty actions of creation. In this way, the Maya maintained a balanced view of time that acknowledged both the sacred and mundane aspects of each day.

There is much information available on how the Maya meshed these two calendars and how they charted and prophesied enormous cycles of time and consciousness. I invite you to research this topic on your own and draw your own conclusions, because I am not going to deal with that here. To be very clear: I am not proposing that my interpretation of the calendar is the definitive version. I believe that just as creation evolves, the way we interpret creation must evolve. What I am focusing on here, and what I have elicited the First Shamans to help me with, is a current interpretation of the sacred twenty-day calendar of creation that we can use to help realign ourselves with creation during this time of great transformation we are living in.

What I *am* suggesting is that we take the ancient knowledge of people that understood the importance of living with a sacred as well as a civil calendar and adapt that knowledge to have meaning in our lives—to help us in our transformation away from greed and power and toward balance and peace.

For this reason, I am not going to try and "tell you" what day it is today in the sacred calendar. If you are interested in the subject of agreeing on days, you can easily find information in books and on the Internet about different calculations and tables that correlate our Gregorian calendar with the Mayan calendar. There may be a time when all people will agree on what day it is within a sacred calendar. This would be a monumental achievement for humanity. But it seems that right now we are still not yet ready for that.

What the First Shamans are indicating is that we first get back on track by aligning our individual talents with creation, and in that way we raise the collective consciousness so that we start to agree with each other as to how to collectively align our human actions with the seemingly timeless actions of creation happening naturally all around us.

Right now we are being asked at a personal level to wake up, to transform, and that is why the resurrection of a personal, sacred calendar of creation is important to be used as a tool on a daily basis in the course of our daily lives. This implies that our sacred calendar be much more than a simple device for marking the name and number of a particular day. The sacred calendar of creation inspires divine actions to be included in what we do with our day. This is how the ancient and modern day Maya use the sacred calendar as well.

So, when relating to the sacred calendar, it is important to view it by the actions of creation that it inspires. Many researchers of the Maya, as well as popular authors who write about the spiritual practices of the Maya, tend to "translate" the names and symbols of the twenty days of the sacred calendar into common names and then base the meaning of the day entirely on the literal translation. For example, the literal translation for the word *Batz'* is "monkey" and *Ix* is "jaguar." But to Mayan shaman/priests, the words used to "name" each of the twenty days are not translatable in the context of assigning them to a fixed set of symbols, beings, or items. The twenty sacred days of the calendar are based on complex actions of creation.

The Maya have specific actions associated with each day, or "Day Lord," as they are commonly referred to. When speaking of a specific day, they address the day in divine fashion by assigning the title Lord to the day, such as "Greetings, Lord Batz'." However, the First Shamans have made it very clear that we are to make our sacred calendar meaningful for our lives today and the fashion in which we live, so to simply copy the Mayan sacred calendar or try to apply their actions to our lives would not only be impractical but would also be disrespectful. That is why I have taken the clues and instructions from the Maya and then updated the information to include acts of creation pertinent to our modern lives.

The Mayan "Long Count" calendar ends sometime around the year 2012; the Long Count is an extremely complex version of the Mayan calendar for tracking vast periods of time. If we take this as a sign of the next great evolution in consciousness, then our sacred calendar must be based on actions that lead us in that direction. This is what has been indicated by the First Shamans and what I have laid out in this chapter. The time has come for us to stop treating our Mother Earth only as something we need to care for to ensure our survival. What we are being asked for now is to co-create a world of peace and joy with our Mother.

Using the Calendar

The first step in integrating the sacred calendar into our lives in a meaningful way is to personally align ourselves with creation. There is no one who can tell you where you currently stand in relation to creation; that is a relationship between you and creation. The one thing that we all have is a unique perspective of the world and where we fit in. That is what gives us our individuality and consciousness of being conscious. Therefore, the task of initiating yourself with the Day Lords, or Day Creators as I prefer to acknowledge them, rests solely with you. So the day you choose to begin your work with the calendar is completely up to you.

However, I have found that once a person gets to the point of awakening where they are inspired to relate their days with the Day Creators, that day is usually a day of Ak'abal, a day of fresh potential, of new beginnings. For this reason, I have placed Ak'abal at the beginning of the list below. Once you have reviewed the descriptions of the twenty Day Creators, then it's time to find out which Day Creator is inspiring your day today. The idea here is to facilitate your alignment with the calendar in whatever way you see fit. Some suggestions would be to go alone for a period of time in nature and just "be" with creation until you feel which Day Creator you are in alignment with. Or you could walk along a busy street, go for a swim in the ocean, or even jump out of a plane. It really doesn't matter what you do as long as you feel clear about what day of creation you are currently aligned with.

Once you align with that Day Creator, the simplest thing to do is write the name of that Day Creator on your Gregorian calendar on today's date, and then each successive Day Creator for the next nineteen days. On the twenty-first day since your beginning, you will once again start with your first Day Creator. For example, if your first day is Ak'abal, your 21st day will be also—and so will your 41st, 61st, and 261st.

Please note that even though I do not find it necessary to correlate our Gregorian calendar with the calculations of Mayan researchers so as to have everyone "agree" on what day it is for everyone on the sacred calendar, I do believe that the Maya understood the patterns of creation as it applied to human consciousness very well, so the order of the procession of the Day Creators is best left in the order that they present it. For example, C'at days follow Ak'abal, the day of Junajpu follows Cawuk, and so on.

Writing the Day Creators' names in succession on your Gregorian calendar is useful from a practical standpoint, simply because it is the calendar that everyone agrees on using and one that we will not be giving up anytime soon. The Maya did the same thing: they used both the business calendar and the sacred calendar. However, if you have arrived at the place in your life where it is not necessary to know on each day what everyone else is agreeing that day is, by all means it is an excellent idea to exclusively use the sacred calendar for short or long periods of time. I have done this on many occasions, and it is an extremely enlightening and liberating way to live in harmony with creation.

When you first begin to use the sacred calendar, it may be that it isn't a dominating force or factor in your life. The hectic pace of modern life, with all of its complex responsibilities and the numerous roles we are asked to play each day, puts many people in the position of evolving gradually into aligning their daily actions with creation. But even if you simply embody the Day Creator for each day upon waking in the morning and do one thing in alignment with creation, you will still be moving toward the transformation of consciousness. The alignment has a cumulative effect, so the longer you practice, the easier it becomes to align.

As your days become more and more in alignment, you will naturally find your daily actions more and more in tune with creation, until you eventually spend little or no time involved in acts of anti-creation. Conscious co-creation with the world then becomes your way of life, and as such, through your daily actions you help in the much-needed transformation of consciousness worldwide.

Listed here are general descriptions of the twenty Day Creators, the key acts of creation that each inspires, and suggestions for things to do on those days to aid in alignment. As you will see, each Day Creator has their own unique characteristics and personality. The suggestions for things to do on each day are simply to get you started, but I do advise that you try them while aligning with the Day Creators before adding additional actions, simply because the actions I have listed have been proven through working with the calendar for long periods of time in a "modern" context and they will get you quickly into the process.

When you begin, many of the actions that the Day Creators encourage may not be easy to fulfill. Re-aligning our human-centered actions with actions implied by the sacred calendar of creation requires us to alter the way we spend our time. The Day Creators ask us on a daily basis to honor, cherish, and participate harmoniously in life with all of creation. They request for us to grow into more mature and balanced beings that are healthy and whole at the physical, mental, environmental, and spiritual levels.

Please note: while working with the Day Creators, you may notice that I have not expounded on, nor do I suggest, those actions of creation that do not inspire conscious co-creation. Even though lying, stealing, and murdering are surely still part of our world, the sacred calendar is for inspiring truth, connection, and peace in a proactive way. On days such as Tz'i', among a few others, the Day Creators do ask us to work on anti-energetic actions, but this is always toward clearing away and working through those types of actions so as to re-align with creation.

Ak'abal

Ak'abal days are like the opening of a flower. The world is full of potential: fresh, new, and bursting with life. A new dawn has come with fresh light to clear away previous obstacles so that new ideas and acts of creation may be born.

acts of creation keywords

dawn, rebirth, opening, unlocking, beginning, initiating, activating

things to do

- Begin a new project or activity in alignment with creation.
- Have a sunrise ceremony in a place that is special to you.
- Visit a place you've always wanted to see.
- Formally remove from your life an energy-draining habit or action of anti-creation.
- Participate in, or make concrete plans to participate in, a powerful ceremony of energetic and psychic cleaning, such as the embrace of the earth ceremony, a fire ceremony, or a vision quest.[14]

---

14 See *Ecoshamanism*, chapter 6.

C'at

This is a day to focus on "squaring up" with the world around you. It is a day of offering, giving, and "paying" for the gifts of life and creation we receive every day. On this day, we intentionally spread light and energy to others, say thank you to those that should be thanked, and ask forgiveness from those we may have hurt.

acts of creation keywords

offering, payment, reconciliation, resolution, reward

things to do

- Make offerings for creation at your altars and shrines.
- Make a donation to a reputable national or international charity, or give something useful to a local homeless or poor person.
- Make an effort to pay debts that you owe to people or businesses.
- Say "thank you" to someone or someplace that helped you, especially someone or someplace you haven't yet thanked for their help.
- Ask forgiveness from someone or someplace that was hurt by your actions.

Can

The energy of Can inspires healing through direct communication with creation. Can days invite us to strengthen our link with creation by cleaning up and organizing our altars so that we then are better able to ward off or cure any illnesses that may be affecting us or someone around us.

acts of creation keywords

curing, healing, clearing, cleaning, refocusing

things to do

- Focus this day on your relationship with the "Three Cs": connection (your skin is not a boundary, it is an organ that connects you to everything around you), communication (honesty with yourself, with others, with your natural environment), and consciousness (your level of being awake is directly proportional to how much of your actions are in alignment with creation).
- Build a new altar or sacred shrine.
- Visit one or more of your altars and shrines and clean them up. For example, take away representations of old offerings, rearrange and dust off sacred items, replace candles, repair structures, etc.
- Intentionally work with your tékas and ask them to help heal you from afflictions of a physical, psychological, spiritual, or environmental nature.
- Do something specific and tangible to help others heal from their afflictions.

Came

Came days are all about getting along. We are asked to bring peace and tranquility into our actions, form partnerships, and be helpful to others. On these days, we pay close attention to being respectful of the natural world and to all beings that share our planet.

acts of creation keywords

peace, tranquility, partnership, marriage, serenity, calmness, silence, diplomacy, counseling

things to do

- Make prayers for peace at your altars and shrines.
- Visit a shrine built by someone else and add your prayers of peace (Buddhist *stupas* are a fine example and are usually easy to locate).
- Focus this day on spreading tranquility and peace to those around you by your peaceful thoughts and actions.
- Practice random acts of kindness with those you meet.
- Help an environmental group or volunteer at a hospital, animal shelter, youth center, etc.

Quej

This is a good day to "get things done," especially with other people. The energy of Quej inspires positive acts of creation concerning public or private meetings, electing leaders, performing blessings, and during graduations or initiations.

acts of creation keywords

communication, cooperation, collaboration, teamwork

things to do

- Participate in a community event, public meeting, or some other type of activity that brings people together for common goals.
- Initiate a community event, public meeting, or some other type of activity that brings people together for common goals.
- Conduct or participate in some type of public or group ceremony, ritual, or blessing that is in alignment with creation.

K'anil

This is a day of both learning and sharing what you know. If the time is right, K'anil is a good day to pass down information to younger generations or students. At the same time, it is also a good day for receiving such information. In this way, K'anil is a day with much power for teachers, shamans, mentors, etc.

acts of creation keywords

teaching, learning, planting, feeding, growing, sharing, inspiring

things to do

- Intentionally pass knowledge to, or spend time with, someone (including children) who will make good use of something positive you have to share.
- Open yourself to learning something new from someone, someplace, or forces both seen and unseen around you.
- Take time to read something that you have wanted to read, or sit down and write if you are inspired to do so.
- Help someone get started on a new phase in their life.

Toj

The essence of Toj is the duality of balance. It is a very yin/yang day that makes us aware of light and dark, hot and cold, borrowing and paying back, hard work and laziness, selfless acts and selfish acts. On this day, pay attention to how there is no shadow without light, no men without women, no day without night.

acts of creation keywords

balance, duality, symmetry, counterpart, complement

things to do

- This is a great day for counterpractice (see chapter 9).
- Pay close attention to the phenomenon of "reflections" in water, on glass, in peoples' eyes.
- "See" deeper into the cycles and systems around you that you are part of. For example, pay attention to all the things that turning on a light switch connects you to[15] all the people and places you affect with your purchases. Recognize that trees live as much below the ground as above, that the act of breathing in and out connects you to everything around you, etc.

---

15 See chapter 3 of *Ecoshamanism*.

Tz'i'

Tz'i' is a day for acknowledging and working on any fears, doubts, or energy-draining situations in your life. Instead of continuing to avoid these things, join with the energy of Tz'i' toward resolving them.

acts of creation keywords

personal growth, intuition, insight, overcoming, prevailing

things to do

- Make a list of things in your life you have been avoiding because you are afraid or simply don't know how to resolve them. On Tz'i' days, work with the energy of this Day Creator to come up with strategies on how to deal with these difficult situations in your life.

- Because this day is about facing fears and doubts, be especially careful in your actions. Be intentionally aware to avoid carelessness and avoid any energy-draining habits that could make you weaker or susceptible to "bad luck." On Tz'i' days, we must really make a big effort to overcome our weaknesses, and when we do, we continue to feel the positive effects of our efforts throughout the next nineteen days.

Batz'

Batz' days are very life-affirming and productive. They are good days for traveling, business deals, creating art, and constructing.

acts of creation keywords

production, creation, invention, commerce

things to do

- Dedicate time to doing what you love, especially if you don't take the time to do it very often.
- Evaluate how you currently provide for yourself and/or your dependants, and make decisions relating to necessary changes.
- Bring forth your artistic qualities and create something from your heart.
- Actively engage important people in different areas of your life (family, business, school, organizations, etc.) in conversations that lead to strengthening your relationships and making them as efficient as possible.
- Visit places that make you feel good, or be adventurous and go somewhere new and exciting.

E

The energy of E awakens us to the mystical aspects of life and numinous mysteries. E days are good for formally beginning a new stage of life or discovering the need for a change in what we are doing. Feasts and celebrations are also common on E days, for those events that honor the sacredness of life and the service of conscious co-creation.

acts of creation keywords

awakening to your current task in life, celebrating the sacred, acknowledging the mystical qualities of life

things to do

- Engage in an activity that opens you to discovering your current task in life or that helps affirm and support the fulfillment of your task, if you already know it.
- E is another powerful day for the building and honoring of shrines and assessing how your daily actions are or aren't in alignment with conscious co-creation.
- Hold a feast or a celebration to honor the joy of life, embarking on a new task, or a new phase in your life or in the life of someone else.

Aj

Aj days are good for taking care of things around the house and paying special attention to children, relatives, pets, and animals. It is a nurturing day, filled with feelings of support and stability. Aj also inspires us to take care of or even pamper our physical body.

acts of creation keywords

home life, nurturing, devotion, care, attentiveness, love

things to do

- Take care of any domestic responsibilities around your house that you've been avoiding.
- Spend time with a loved one or a good friend you haven't seen in a while.
- Do something special at home with your kids, loved ones, or pets.
- Care for your garden or other living things around your house.
- Get a massage or pamper your physical body in some way.
- Take the time to make yourself and your loved ones a special meal.

Ix

Ix days are dedicated to the spirits of nature (the Kakaiyeri). On these days, it is good to honestly assess your relationship with nature and your actions of creation or anti-creation, make offerings, and ask forgiveness of nature if necessary. Spend as much time outdoors on these days as possible, while communing with the more-than-human worlds of nature and spirit.

acts of creation keywords

aligning with nature, communing with and honoring the spirit of our Mother Earth

things to do

- Intentionally spend time in a natural setting.
- Review your level of connection to the natural world.
- Ask the spirits of nature to help you with the challenges in your life, and offer them something positive in return.

Tz'iquin

This is a day of preparation to help ensure abundance on a material level for such things as food, shelter, money, etc. It is also a day to be particularly aware of staying away from people that may be cruel or unkind to you.

acts of creation keywords

preparation, abundance, comfort, providing

things to do

- Tz'iquin are good days to focus on the "seasonal" realities of life. Prepare clothes, ready tools, and perform maintenance on items for the upcoming season.
- Make preparations for your garden relating to the season: planting, harvesting, storing.
- Put away some money or goods for a rainy day.

Ajmac

Ajmac is a day of atonement between yourself, others, or the world. Although Ajmac is a serious day, that does not necessarily mean it is a somber day; atonement can be a joyous occasion as well. Ajmac is also a day to be especially aware of ways you may be wasteful and how to live more sustainably.

acts of creation keywords

atonement, crying, laughing, recycling, salvaging, reusing

things to do

- Focus on ways you can "tread more lightly" in your actions with the world. Devise strategies for inviting more balance and peace in your life and in the world.
- Intentionally practice the "Three Rs": reduce, recycle, reuse.
- In general, emotionally atone with the world around you.

No'j

The essence of No'j is thought. On No'j days, it is good to contemplate how our thoughts influence our actions of both conscious co-creation and intentional or unintentional destructive behavior.

acts of creation keywords

intelligence, consciousness, contemplation, cleverness, stupidity, thoughtlessness

things to do

- While Ajmac is an emotional day, No'j is more mental. It is a good day for intellectual research into topics of interest for you or for the tasks in your life that you are working on.
- Stimulate your mind with books or topics that normally feel too academic or dry. On No'j days, the Day Creator helps us to move past our self-imposed limitations on an intellectual level.
- Analyze how the consensus of thought between large numbers of people affects the way you act and how your actions might be different if you were to allow yourself to govern your own day.

Tijax

This day is about conflict and resolution. On a Tijax day, be especially aware of how you handle conflicts in your life and what major conflicts are happening in the world and how they are being resolved. Reflect on how you handle, or would handle, people who would persecute you or take from you unjustly.

acts of creation keywords

resolution, change, forgiveness, morality, sacrifice, equality

things to do

- Intentionally practice *In Lak'ech* (see chapter 9).
- Watch or read the news, and be aware of how far from the practice of *In Lak'ech* our world is right now.
- Throughout your day, honestly look at how you deal with conflict and resolution in your own life.

Cawuk

The energy of Cawuk inspires us to nurture and work on projects already started. Just as a trip has a beginning and an end, the middle part of the journey must be carried out in a mindful way. Cawuk is the energy of creation that gets us from start to finish, from asleep to awake, from A to B.

acts of creation keywords

motion, inspiration, energy, action, activity

things to do

- Tackle a challenging aspect of a current project with increased energy and enthusiasm as well as the knowledge that *you can do it*. Go for it!
- Revitalize yourself by doing something physically active. If you are accustomed to exercise, then do something physically different and challenging.
- Ask for help from other people, if necessary, to help move along a current project. Feel good about asking by also offering to help them with something in return.

Junajpu

Junajpu relates to learning from our ancestors about how to live today. This involves looking at both our previous successes and failures, life and death, health and sickness. Junajpu inspires us to evolve into more awakened beings in alignment with creation by making us take a closer look at death.

acts of creation keywords

awareness of death, learning from our past, time, cycles, transformation

things to do

- Create or visit an ancestor shrine (see chapter 6).
- Throughout your day, reflect on how short our time in this body really is. Do not focus on the inevitable, but rather let that awareness inspire you to not put off for a possibly nonexistent tomorrow the things that you could do today.
- Reflect on the ways that you have already transformed in your life, then look forward to see where you are heading next.

Imo:x

On Imo:x days, we intentionally appreciate that we are in the midst of a mysterious and magical existence on one tiny planet in an incomprehensibly vast omniverse. We are humbled by the knowledge of how little we truly know. Imo:x also makes us aware of how unwise it is to go against creation. This is a good day to humbly visit sacred sites and acknowledge the immense powers of creation that we are just a small part of.

acts of creation keywords

humility, consciousness, mindfulness, respect, reverence, awe

things to do

- Create and use an altar of center (see chapter 6).
- Visit altars, shrines, and sacred places at night under the stars and relate to them while looking into the sky and acknowledging how incomprehensibly vast is creation.
- Use the times of sunrise and sunset to inspire awe in the mysteriousness of creation.

Ik'

Ik' days are for the awareness of power, power in the forces of nature that are strong enough to cause hurricanes, earthquakes, volcanoes, etc., and the power of human beings to create nuclear weapons, spaceships, genetically altered plants and animals, etc. On Ik' days, we are asked to examine how we are using our personal power and what we are creating.

acts of creation keywords

power, force, natural "catastrophes," intense emotions, energy, awareness, examination, assessment

things to do

- Make a list of what you have created since the last Ik' day (especially what you have created with what you do for "work"). Add to that list the processes of anti-creation you have shared in (buying and using fossil fuels, nuclear-powered electricity, etc.).

- Visit the site of a powerful creation, either natural (visit the ocean, climb a mountain, go to the site of a recent forest fire or severe storm, etc.) or humanmade (visit a landfill, inner-city slum, architectural masterpiece, library, etc.). Assess your emotions and feelings while at these sites, and ask yourself why you feel the way you do.

- During the course of your day, pay attention to the uses of "power" everywhere around you.

Chapter 8

Reclaiming, Raising, and Wisely Using Personal Energy

"Grandfather, I am very intrigued with how modern science is now confirming many of the previously scoffed-at beliefs and practices of shamans and mystics. Although I don't properly understand all of the complex thinking behind the new physics of quantum theory, what seems to be being said is that the ancients seers were actually right the whole time: matter and consciousness are a continuum. And that the universe is created by the participation of those who participate."

Is there a question somewhere in there, hijo?

"Well, I guess I have intuitively known this for a long time, but I would like to learn more about how we can use this knowledge in a practical way. It's easy to see how matter affects consciousness, but if consciousness and matter are a continuum, then consciousness can affect matter in the same way. I understand how this can be seen in the practices of healers that work at an energetic level. But can this knowledge be used at a practical level in the course of our everyday lives?"

Seveneenth-century repre-
sentation of the third-eye
connection to the universal
consciousness, by alchemist
Robert Fludd. (Image: http://
en.wikipedia.org/wiki/Image:
RobertFuddBewusstsein17Jh.
png)

Of course! And if you were to do that, there would be no need for these "energy healers" you speak of. This word—"energy"—is very tricky, because it refers to the spark of creation. Learning to use "your" energy in alignment with creation is what we have been talking about all along. So of course the knowledge of consciousness and matter as a continuum can be used in your daily life. Your consciousness affects matter at the most personal of levels: your level of energy and the way you relate to your "physical" body, your actions with those around you, and the manner in which you relate to your environment.

"So when sometimes I feel like I have more energy at a physical or mental level than at other times, that is a result of consciousness relating to matter?"

That would be one way to say it. Another way would simply be to say that your level of energy is directly influenced by consciousness. You don't have much to say about the quantity of energy you are born with, but you certainly can consciously and even unconsciously affect your energy "level," which is what you "feel."

"Yes, I realize that people are born with different levels of energy, depending on the circumstances of their conception, the energy level of the parents, and the position of the sun and moon at the time of creation. But what ultimately determines a person's level of energy is how they use the energy they have been given. Many times, a person born with high energy has an easier time becoming 'successful,' but for that very reason they squander their energy away and actually end up worse off than a person born with lower energy who has used it wisely. But I'm not clear about what you mean by unconsciously affecting energy levels."

You have to think bigger, that's all.

Answer this question: when you are dreaming, where is your consciousness?

You could be dreaming that you are having dinner with some friends. But in your dream, the division between "yourself," the other people, and the food you prepared is just an illusion. Everything in your dream is subordinate to the unconscious state of "your" consciousness. You cannot "physically" separate the items of your dream.

Now we ask: when you are awake, where is your consciousness?

The typical answer would be "inside my head." But when neurosurgeons cut into the human brain, searching for consciousness, they don't find it—because it is not a "thing." Consciousness is an action of creation that touches and is part of everything. Mind and matter are simply different vibrations, or ripples, in the same pool. When a pebble is dropped into a pool of water, it affects the entire pool. Your "unconscious" dreams affect how you feel when you awake, just as your conscious actions affect how you dream. Freudian thoughts conjure Freudian dreams conjuring Freudian actions. Thoughts about conscious co-creation conjure dreams of co-creating that inspire actions of co-creation.

"Okay, I get it. Everything is connected, so my unconscious dreams affect my energy in the same way as my conscious thoughts and actions."

Now we can go one step further. If you were born with a certain level of energy, what is it that dictates your current level?

"The way I use my energy during my life."

Exactly. But realize that this can mean many different things at different levels. For example, your nutritional intake can affect your level of physical energy, but just as important is your mental state. If two men of equal strength are climbing a mountain, and one is feeling happy about the adventure and excited to get to the top and the other is feeling sorry for himself and worried because he just lost his job, which do you think is going to have more available energy? That's right, the one that is not dragging the emotional ball and chain.

To take this further, you must realize that in many cases people continue for many years, or even their whole lives, giving away their energy to past emotional events. Reclaiming this energy by stopping these draining conscious and unconscious emotional responses is key to influencing your level of energy and how you feel.

"What you are saying is that when we feel hurt about some situation, we give away energy in the form of emotional responses, and then we continue to drain energy thereafter if we do not stop our emotional attachment to the event. But when we are able to let go of it, we are then making more efficient use of the energy we possess. In this way, we are not 'raising' our level of energy, but we feel more energetic because we now have more energy available since we are not wasting it."

That is correct, but to do this properly you do not just "let go of it." You must heal these drains, and that requires more effort than merely forgetting or denying. Someone or some situation that caused you harm twenty years ago may well be responsible for your initial injury. But if it is still hurting you all this time later, who is responsible for those twenty years of lost energy? You are. You can't go back in time and change the event, but you sure can change how you relate to the event and how much energy you continue to feed it. And don't forget that you not only waste energy on past events, but on worrying about the future as well. Being clear and present so as to reclaim energy-draining attachments to the past or the future, increasing your energy by plugging into higher sources, and maintaining a high level of available energy through conscious living are the three key aspects of what you are asking about.

"Please tell me more about plugging into higher sources."

This is all about relating to creation as an interconnected continuum of matter and consciousness, just as you previously described. The "higher sources" are already a part of you and influence your life at every level and in every moment. They are but ripples in the same pond. It is your relationship to these "elements" that determines how they affect you. For example, your Mother Earth has a very special relationship with the star of your solar system, just as you do. Even if you are not conscious of how special this relationship is, you are still affected by it in every moment of your life. But when you heal your energy drains, become conscious of your Luminous Self, and align your actions with creation, your relationship toward the sun transforms as the ripples become waves.

"I think what you are saying is that energy sources such as the sun are not necessarily higher sources since they are all part of the continuum, but they are bigger fields or concentrations of the energies of creation, and that if we enhance our relationship with these concentrations, it affects us at every level. I have felt this with not only the sun but also bodies of water, wind in the valleys and tops of mountains, the great body of Earth in so many moments, and especially with you, Grandfather."

Yes … yes … now keep going …

"Well, I have also felt connected to a 'higher' source as I have developed special relationships with animals, birds, and trees. These relationships don't feel the same as when I connect to the sun, but they definitely energize me and make me aware of the interconnectedness of all life."

Very good. But you are still forgetting something very important …

"Of course! Other people! Through living the Luminous Self, I have certainly felt connected and energized during relationships with other human beings …"

This is the lesson for you, hijo. You have already developed your abilities in connecting with the essences and energies of the "natural" world. You even wrote a 300-page book about it to share with your people. Now it is time you realize at a deeper level that in this time of trans-

formation in consciousness, you must also develop your abilities in connecting the energies of the Luminous Self with other people as well. Imagine what the world would be like if everyone lived In Lak'ech, if everyone lived the Luminous Self. This starts one person at a time, hijo. But then it enlarges by small groups intentionally joining, then larger and larger groups, until there is a critical mass that evokes change.

Practice:
reclaiming lost energy by healing energetic drains

Energetic drains take real effort to deal with because they come in so many different varieties. For most of us, if we were to sit and think for a few moments and come up with present, past, and future situations in our life that would classify as energy draining, there would be a number that immediately come to mind. These would be the first ones to work on. But there are also those events and situations that we don't want to admit to ourselves as being energy draining. And of course we also have events from the past that we "block out" in an attempt to not be hurt by them any longer.

The good news is that once you begin to work on energetic drains that you are presently conscious of, the increase in available energy saved by healing those drains actually helps you to discover and deal with those "undercover" drains that were previously hidden or that you were avoiding because you didn't have the energy available to deal with them.

There are numerous techniques in dealing with energy drains. One effective technique is "recapitulation." Recapitulation was brought into the Western world predominantly by the writing of Carlos Castaneda, and then later by Victor Sanchez, who refined the technique through working with large groups of people over a period of many years. Having worked very closely with Victor, and having spent many months engaged in intense recapitulation, I can attest to its effectiveness. Victor's specific technique is covered in his book *The Toltec Path of Recapitulation: Healing Your Past to Free Your Soul.*

The basis behind recapitulation, as well as other techniques dealing with energy drains, is that you intentionally engage in healing them by identifying, patching, and then healing them. To illustrate this, I'll run through a few examples using a technique adapted from teachings by my Wirrarika mentors.

In this technique, Grandfather Fire is brought in to help inspire, facilitate, and purify. In all cases when working with the fire, I prefer to be outdoors with an actual wood fire made in a sacred way, but with significant intention, a simple candle can be used effectively.

The first stage is identifying energetic drains at mental, physical, environmental, and spiritual levels. Here is a short list of a few:

mental drains

- negative thinking
- impatience
- superficial relationships
- repetitive thoughts / actions
- unresolved conflicts with people
- avoiding the forgiveness of others
- inability to ask for forgiveness
- trying to "keep up" with the neighbors

physical drains

- eating unhealthy foods
- misplacing emotional needs by treating your body poorly
- not getting sufficient rest
- not providing your body with exercise to keep it healthy
- paying too much attention to your physical appearance
- avoiding medical and dental issues
- spending day after day at a job that is physically unhealthy or overly sedentary

environmental drains

- stress about where you live and / or wanting to move
- transportation and household items in need of repair
- clutter and disorganization

- unreturned phone calls and emails
- missing being part of a supportive community
- lack of beauty or inspiring surroundings
- noise and too much television
- feeling overwhelmed by all the information you are bombarded with every day

spiritual drains

- missing quality friendships
- missing romantic partners
- being in a relationship that compromises your values
- not making the time to release and nurture your creative energy
- lack of activities that feed your spiritual nature
- clinging to outdated or intolerant spiritual beliefs

In reviewing the complexity of modern life, we can easily see that this is a short list of energy-draining possibilities. Having spent many years working with people in this technique with the fire, two broad categories are almost always present. The first is the energy-draining circumstance of tolerating dysfunction. This happens on physical and environmental levels as we avoidingly tolerate ugliness, distracting noises, growing waistlines, lack of communication, inefficient processes, and wasteful activities. Taken individually, these things may seem rather minor, but when combined, the energy-draining stress of dysfunction can result in a significant decrease in available energy.

Another major energy-draining circumstance is when we take care of ourselves last. In other words, while providing for loved ones or fulfilling other types of obligations feels satisfying and may be quite necessary, it also requires energy. If we continue to give our energy after we are already running low, not only do we risk health issues but also feelings of resentment and animosity may set in, which are major energy drainers and only make the situation worse. Taking the required time to take care of ourselves makes us more efficient when taking care of the things in our life.

Reclaiming energy in this technique begins by identifying the energy drainers I have listed above, as well as the others I have not, that are a part of your current life. Writing them down is the first step. You can list them in the manner I have above or group them into other categories, such as:

- My relationships
- My body
- My work
- My money
- My home
- My thoughts
- My spirit
- My natural environment

And so on. Once you have your list, sit or stand in front of the fire and "confess" your energy-draining actions to the fire. Use your voice for this—don't try to use telepathy. Speaking clearly, out loud, will help you to project and move energy. If you have trusted companions to witness you do this, even better.

After the confession, choose two or three energy-draining actions that you feel confident you can heal. You want to make sure you have a good chance of healing these, because once you do you will have more available energy for healing others. Don't go straight for the biggest ones—for example, if you are a long-time smoker and have tried to quit many times before. You probably didn't have sufficient available energy to do it simply because of all the other, smaller energy drains you have. By fixing the smaller ones first, you will then have the energy available for dealing with a major one, like a long-term addiction. Healing energy drains has a snowball effect. The more you heal, the more momentum is gathered for continued healing.

Next, choose your first energy-draining action, state it out loud, and while looking into the flames "see" yourself doing the action as if watching yourself in a movie. For example, if the situation you have chosen is your messy office, then see yourself in different moments when you have created the clutter.

Now, shift your perspective and relive moments in your messy office. Be there by seeing through your eyes and reliving how it feels in that space.

After reliving this situation, shift your awareness back to being with the fire, and make a commitment to resolving this issue and the time period it will take you. State it out loud.

In the flames, visualize the outcome of your positive energy action. In this example, you will see your office clean and organized.

The last step is to give your energy-draining action to the fire and ask for help in completing your task. Typically, giving to the fire is with fuel, so in this case you could write the energy-draining situation down on a small piece of paper and feed it to the fire while asking for support.

Once you have completed the task(s), you have only "patched" the energy drain. It will be your continued vigilance that will keep the patch on until you have fully healed. For example, just because you cleaned your office doesn't mean it will stay clean. Use the fire or a candle flame to stay connected with your energy-draining commitments.

Obviously, the above example is small when compared to emotional trauma or physical-abuse events, but these events can be dealt with in the same way. In this example, if you have been feeling guilty for not making amends with a deceased loved one before they passed away, you would see yourself in the flames interacting with that person, then you would relive your experiences, then you would ask forgiveness or ask to be forgiven or whatever else needs to be said (do this out loud, just as if they were sitting there with you), then make a decision and a commitment with regard to this situation. For example, the patch would be to deal with a situation with a loved one whom you have been avoiding. To fully heal from this, you commit with the fire from now on to say what needs to be said in the moment it needs saying.

To be truly effective with this technique, you will need to use all your creativity and resources. Start small and begin healing the drains that are easier to accomplish. Once you do this, you will feel an increase in available energy, and that energy will help you to conquer your more difficult energy-draining thoughts and habitual actions.

Here are some tips and additional considerations that may help you when using this technique:

- Seeing yourself like a movie in your energy-draining situation is fairly easy for most people, but shifting your awareness into the energy-draining situation in order to relive it is tricky until you get a feel for it. To help, you can practice doing this with all kinds of positive situations. Consciously and energetically relive special moments in your life, beautiful places you have been, etc., until you get a good feel for the process of "reliving."

- Coming up with commitments for patching energy drains will sometimes take a fair amount of creativity and maybe more than one session with the fire. For example, if you constantly worry about money problems, a solution to this may not be readily apparent. First, ask the fire, and use the sacred flame to help you with insights. Then be open to receiving answers, especially answers that may not be the most comfortable to accept. Then, if you still don't see a solution, work on other energy drains first. Once your available energy has increased, you will be able to work through any problem you face.

- Moving from patching to truly healing a major energy drain requires a sound strategy. You must come up with a legitimate plan of action that will keep you on a healthy energetic path. For example, patching an energetic drain caused by someone physically abusing you may include being able to forgive that person, reclaiming the energy you have lost to that situation, and helping other abused people. But truly healing from that event might later be helped by intentionally creating healthy relationships with others or engaging in random acts of kindness with the people around you (even if they don't know you're doing something nice for them) so that you counteract the effects of the injury.

- Don't get down on yourself if a patch comes off. Energetic healing can be a time-consuming and challenging process with both successes and failures. This is one of the main reasons to use the sacred flame. In moments of doubt and weakness, go to the fire and feel the numinous energy throughout your whole being. Gain strength from this ancient energy and then continue on your path.

Practice:
raising our amount of available energy through connecting with the energetic sources of nature

This happens at the most effective level once we have dealt with habitual energy drains and have an abundance of energy available to explore new ways of perception. Typically, people spend a vast majority of their energy just "getting through" the day, which doesn't leave much for other types of activities that add magic and mystery to life. But when we have awakened enough to deal with our energy expenditures in a healthy way, we realize that energetic interaction with the world around us need not be draining at all. In fact, there are even ways of being that raise more energy than is being expended.

The first step in this process is having the available energy to increase your ability to use all of your senses—to perceive in a way that integrates information and energy across senses, through time and space. At this level of perception, the world is an energetic wonderland just waiting to be explored.

Studies now indicate that most people in our country now spend an incredible 90 percent of their lives indoors. This takes a large toll on the ability to use even our most basic senses. In many cases, we have simply lost the knowledge of how to perceive what is naturally occurring in nature. But we all have the capacity to reverse this situation, and as we reclaim available energy by patching and healing drains, we now have the time and energy to reconnect with nature and the more-than-human world. When this happens, we move way past seeing the countryside as merely beautiful scenery. We intentionally meld our awareness and perception into the continuum of consciousness and matter to become one with the natural world and all of creation.

What we call our "senses" are typically referred to as the physiological methods of how we perceive the world. And this is a good starting point in understanding, but it is certainly not the whole story in terms of perception. Limiting our perceptual abilities to five senses—sight, touch, taste, hearing, and smell—is a completely inadequate and antiquated way of describing the abilities of human beings to perceive. Awakened researchers, such as Dr. Michael Cohen, who for many years has been conducting ecopsychological studies with groups of people engaged in activities of reconnecting with nature, have confirmed the notion that we have many abilities to perceive in ways beyond these five basic senses. In his research, Cohen actually lists fifty-three human senses![16]

By actively engaging our multi-sensory capacities, we become more evolved and awakened human beings who are much more sensitive than when living in a cocoon of strictly human affairs. In my previous books, I have written widely about techniques of reconnecting with nature. One of my favorite energetic practices from *Earthwalks for Body and Spirit* involves intentionally receiving the numinous qualities of energy from the sun. Shamanic techniques for raising energy by direct connection with concentrated energies, such as sun, water, wind, soil, trees, and plants, can be found in *Ecoshamanism* with such practices as sacred fire initiation, the breaths of power, honoring the hydro-logic cycle, and the embrace of the earth ceremony, among many others.

Practice:
the embrace of the earth ceremony

(The complete ceremony is included in chapter 6 of *Ecoshamanism*. This brief overview of the ceremony is included here as an example of a shamanic technique that fully engages people with their Mother in a transformative way.)

The key aspects to this rite of passage are the purification, heightened awareness, and visionary experiences fostered through spending one whole night (or longer) embraced by the earth in a gravelike tomb that is dug by hand into the living soil. The experience of ceremonially digging your own gravelike tomb and being buried in the ground overnight has been described by many that have passed through the ritual as a combination vision quest and full-body meditation. It feels like returning to the womb of your true mother to reclaim that mystical union where all of your hurts are purged and absorbed into the immense physical body and energy of the earth, and then being birthed once again into the light of the world to walk a life path infused with the unconditional love and spiritual guidance of the earth.

When performed with proper preparation and in the appropriate manner, the structure of this rite of passage provides an extremely safe and potent opportunity to touch

---

16 Michael Cohen, *Reconnecting with Nature: Finding Wellness Through Restoring Your Bond with the Earth* (Minneapolis, MN: Ecopress, 1997).

an ecoshamanic state of consciousness that has the power to change your life. Even if you were to simply prepare for the rite, dig and enter your tomb, and then fall asleep for the whole night, you would still be changed. There is no way that one can pass through this rite without being transformed to some degree. However, if you genuinely enter the experience and follow the time-tested suggestions for distilling the most from the rite, the transformational aspects and opportunities for growth and knowledge are limitless.

The embrace of the earth rite of passage is paradoxically very straightforward and extremely complex. The physical side of the ritual is quite simple, and once you learn and understand the logistics you can quickly become comfortable and at ease with the physical aspects of what you are doing and how to do it properly and safely. However, on the mental, psychic, and spiritual levels, the range and complexity of possible experiences prohibits one from knowing or predicting what will actually occur in those realms. As with all shamanic activities, except for the general framework, the internal dynamics of this rite of passage are almost indescribable using words.

During this rite of passage you will pass through five "gates" or stages. The first gate is reviewing and acknowledging your life and what has led you to the moment of this ceremony. During the two-night, three-day version of this rite, the participants tell their life story to the fire and their companions either in one group or separate groups, depending on how many people are participating. Recounting your life out loud in front of a sacred fire and other people, and listening while others do it in front of you, is a powerful exercise that has numerous benefits in terms of personal growth and raising awareness. For the shortened version of the rite, and for those not participating as part of a group, I suggest that you write down the story of your life in the weeks prior to going into the earth. This important step helps you to discover patterns in your behavior so that you can develop strategies to break free from the unwanted ones, and it places your life into a context so that you clearly see where you are in the current moment of your life and how that relates to being buried alive in the earth.

Whether you tell your life story with a group during the rite or you write it down beforehand, the most important preparation for this rite is simply to become clear about why you are doing this, or to at least start the process of this knowing. Some of the reasons may be very apparent, but some may only become clear as you proceed through the process. One of the main tasks of preparation before and during the ceremony will be the finding and clarifying of those parts of yourself and your life to be placed into the forefront of the earth's energy. Below is a short list of circumstances that are appropriate for this rite of passage, followed by brief comments on how to prepare for those that pertain to you:

Obtain clarity and vision in personal matters. This is one of the most readily available gifts of the burial, but in order to get the most from it I suggest that you enter the earth with a short list of very specific questions to pose during your time in the ground. The more to the point the question, the clearer will be the answer. During the days prior to the burial, work on this list and refine it until the time of the ceremony.

Recharge personal energy before or after a demanding task or challenge. The burial into living soil can be a significant activity for preparing energetically and emotionally for a big life event, and/or for recuperating from such an event. The burial places your energy firmly into the reality of the organic world. It cuts through all the technological conveniences of the modern era and allows your energy to mix with the energy of the earth in a pure and intentional way. All that is needed for sharing energy with the land is for you to be relaxed and have an open heart and mind. Make whatever preparations and ask any questions you need in order to promote a peaceful and receptive state of being.

Heal and absorb emotional wounds. Emotional wounds can never be healed by burying them deep inside of your heart or head. They must be brought out and set free. The burial is the perfect place for this, and Earth will accept whatever you need to set free. She won't judge or condemn you, and she will always be there. If you need emotional healing, prepare by writing down and clarifying those specific events that hurt you so that you can bring them out and release them while in the ground.

Mark a significant life change and rite of passage. The embrace of the earth rite has proven to be an extremely valuable tool when passing through a significant time of transition in your life. Make sure to spend time alone with yourself and write down what you want to manifest in your new life and why. Then write down the small steps you will take in order to get there. Take this with you into the womb of Earth and use the experience to mark the moment and obtain vision.

Bury the "old" self and allow the birth of the new. Obviously, digging and spending the night in a gravelike tomb does hold implications of the awareness of death. This can be used in a nonmorbid way in order to give renewed energy, urgency, and strength to your actions. Although you are not placed in any physical danger during the burial, the near-death implications of being buried alive will help you to not put off the things in your life that would be better done today.

Experience in a tangible way the profound love and healing energy of Earth. If there were no other reasons for intentional burial, I would do it simply because it is an extremely potent way to feel physically, psychically, and spiritually our profound connection with the organic soil and the spirit of Earth. Prepare to feel this by acknowledging the daily gifts of life Earth provides us with during the days prior to the burial. If you have time, go to a place in nature and talk to the land about your current life.

In this rite of passage, we intentionally pursue circumstances that bring out from within us the transformational power that is fostered through metaphorically dying and being reborn. But unlike other spiritual forms of this process, where the metaphor is drawn up through words or commitments of being born again, in this ecoshamanic ritual we actually dig our grave and submerge ourselves in it, thereby facing our mortality with the entirety of our human organism. This is about as close as you can get to the awareness of death without placing yourself in mortal danger or having a physical near-death experience. Plus, in this ritual context you are totally submerged inside of an organic process and provided with the support and encouragement to take the opportunity to make positive use of the experience in a way that improves the quality of your life and happiness.

The initiate climbs into the tomb and the material world is left behind. A threshold to the shamanic world of nature and spirit is crossed. The immediate and familiar support of family, friends, colleagues, pets, accomplishments, failures, and all the trappings and freedoms of everyday life are severed. As the initiate lies down in the tomb, the tomb becomes a sacred chamber consecrated by the concrete action of the initiate to know both self and world in new and improved ways. Lying in the tomb with the entrance being covered by the firekeeper, the flesh of the initiate is formally offered to the body of the earth. In these moments, as the last shovelfuls of soil are being thrown on top of the tomb, the exchange between initiate and Earth begins. Flesh begins to become soil and soil begins to become flesh. All begin to come together as one.

The preparations are over, everyone has left, and now it is just you, the earth, and the journey you are about to take, inside and out. Then the firekeeper opens a fist-size hole in the corner of the roof of your earthly cocoon. You are not trapped and you will not die this night. The air hole ensures that fresh, life-giving air surrounds you and is inside of you. The love of the earth is embracing you. The energy of the fire is protecting you. The rest of your life is waiting for you.

The firekeeper puts their hand through the air hole and into the tomb. As you take their hand in yours, the feelings of life and love, companionship and kinship flow between you. And then the hand is gone. The journey begins ...

Practice:
wisely using personal energy
through conscious living

When we live consciously and through the Luminous Self, we end our energy-draining activities and use our personal energy to create and maintain happy, peaceful lives that foster both personal fulfillment and harmonious relationships. The need for therapies, counseling, and dependence on the advice of others falls away as we turn to our inner sources of knowing and conscious connection to the divine.

In the following chapter, I list some basic techniques for living through the Luminous Self, but in terms of energy usage there is something I would like to share with you here that I have found to be very useful.

Oftentimes during the course of our hectic lives, it is good to remind ourselves of the bigger picture and to also acknowledge the full scope of our abilities and who and what we truly are. Below is a list of five simple acknowledgements, inspired by the writing of Dr. Ilchi Lee, that we can state to ourselves periodically to help us live consciously and through the Luminous Self in every moment.

1. I acknowledge that I am a human being, part of the human community, and I respect the human rights and equality of all people on Earth.

2. I acknowledge that I am a child of the earth, part of the natural community, and I am responsible for nurturing and protecting the health and welfare of my Mother Earth.

3. I acknowledge that I am a spiritual being, a part of the eternal spirit of creation, one and indivisible.

4. I acknowledge that I am a healer, with the strength and the ability to help heal the many illnesses and crises that exist on Earth.

5. I acknowledge that I am an activist, dedicated to making a positive influence in the world.

Chapter 9

Techniques for Living Through the Luminous Self

Techniques for living through the Luminous Self are endless and affect every part of our lives. In this chapter, I have listed a few techniques with regard to the interconnection of all life and the way we treat our environment, other people, and even ourselves.

Practice:
examine the results of your daily actions

During the progression toward living through the Luminous Self and toward conscious co-creation, it is important to review our daily actions from an unbiased perspective to see how much we are living in alignment with creation. One effective technique to help facilitate this is the "man on the moon" perspective.

This technique begins by placing in your mind's eye the photos you have seen of our home planet from space. Picture our round, blue-green planet as if you were standing on the moon, looking from way far away. Now zoom in to your continent,

Earth as viewed from the moon. (Photo: NASA)

then country, then state, then city or town, and finally to the exact location on the planet where you are now.

Once you've done that, zoom back out until you are standing on the moon again, and "see" yourself as one tiny little being on the planet. Now begin to review the things you did today as if you were watching a movie of yourself. After you have begun the movie, ask yourself the following questions while watching yourself as if you were someone else:

1. In terms of how this person (you) interacts with their planet on an environmental level, which and how many of their actions were detrimental to the long-term health of the fragile environment that provides us with life? These actions include usage of nonrenewable resources such as gasoline, oil, and coal ... soil depletion from purchasing chemically treated and fertilized foodstuffs ... deforestation from purchasing beef and using nonrecyled paper products and wood building materials ... continuing to spend the majority of your day engaged in "production" that feeds the unsustainable economic growth marketplace ... and so on.

2. How did this person treat the people around them today?

3. What were their thoughts about other people and their environment? Was this person considerate, peaceful, and compassionate, or selfish, vengeful, and insensitive?

4. How did they feel about themselves and their place in the world?

5. Which and how many of their actions were intentionally done with conscious co-creation in mind?

6. What things could this person change to live more through their Luminous Self and align with creation?

Practice:
don't let the behavior of other people dictate how you feel

Your Luminous Self will not let people who are still hypnotized (but often think they are awake) dictate your feelings, your thoughts, or your actions. Your Luminous Self employs your inherent intuitive and psychic capacities without the need to be openly or secretly codependent on the hypnosis being dealt out by asleep people and their institutions.

Your Luminous Self knows that when asleep people blame or condemn others, it's because they can't help it. Their actions are performed mechanically as a result of their hypnosis. Passively observe yourself (as in the previous practice) and others, and realize that being awake means having a choice that is independent of how others will view it.

Practice:
don't allow any friendship or relationship to require the submission of your luminous self

It may well be that you become awakened to your Luminous Self before many of those around you. Once you begin to shed your old ways and align your actions with creation, those around you will probably resist this "new" you. Don't let them use their hypnotic techniques to put you back to sleep. If they attempt to insist or require that you change back to who you used to be, then it is time to form new relationships with awakened people. It may be that you are required to help awaken those around you, which is fine, but not at the expense of living through your Luminous Self.

Practice:
I understand other people to the exact degree that I understand myself

This is why it is so important to truly awaken. When we live through the Luminous Self, we don't blame ourselves or others for previous actions or present troubles. We understand that our previous actions were from an asleep person who can't be blamed for being asleep, and so we also know that with that understanding also comes the acceptance of other people that act the way we used to.

Practice:
I can only recognize a virtue in another person that I recognize in myself

Just as we become awakened to our previously asleep actions and the asleep actions of those that are still hypnotized, we also recognize the virtues and gifts of others as we allow them to blossom forth from our Luminous Self. As we become conscious co-creators, we experience alignment that leads to balance that leads to peacefulness. The more we experience these states, the more we can recognize these virtues—and the potential for these virtues—in other people.

Practice:
don't act from fears of what others will think of you or even what you will think of yourself

We must dare to awaken our Luminous Self and act from that place, no matter what the short-term consequences. As we are able to understand and not blame those that are hypnotized, and as we begin to perceive the virtues in all of those around us, we become responsible for helping facilitate the awakening of those who are sleep. We do that through example. If we are to lead and teach by example, there is no room for worrying about how our actions will be perceived by those who are still asleep. If we relinquish our intuition and the knowledge gleaned from a clear connection to creation, we have lost the gift of living through the Luminous Self. When we are guided by the Luminous Self, we do not fear how others will perceive our actions, because we "know" our actions are in alignment with creation, even if others don't understand.

Practice:
don't try to be loving, work to be luminous and true; being real is being loving

During this time of transformation in our world, there seems to be many people who are really trying to embrace a loving relationship with those around them. But there is a huge difference in being truly loving and trying to be loving. Once you live through the Luminous Self, it's easy to know when someone is merely portraying love and peace and when someone is actually radiating love and peace. Those who radiate love have discovered their True Self; those that don't are still hypnotized. But understand this: people who radiate love and peace may not appear to those asleep as overly loving or joyous. The Luminous Self radiates love through the expression of actions in alignment with creation, the understanding of the interconnection of all life, and the practice of *In Lak'ech* (see next practice), not by simply acting loving when around others. In practice, when we are true to our Luminous Self we find the source of love inside of us—and when that happens, we no longer "try" to be loving. Our love becomes simply an expression of how we relate to the world.

Practice:
in lak'ech

Those that have studied Mayan cosmology or are familiar with author Hunbatz Men probably already know of this concept, but I invite you to keep reading, as you may not have embraced all the qualities I am describing.

Many of us who live in a Christian-dominated society are familiar with the New Testament's "do unto others as you would have done unto you." Variations of this theme also appear in the Talmud, Koran, and the Analects of Confucius. While this "golden rule" is certainly an awesome suggestion on how to live, the Mayan action of co-creation that in modern times is known simply as *In Lak'ech* goes much deeper and is at the very core of living through the Luminous Self.

Simply put, *In Lak'ech* can be translated as " you are my other self" or "I am another yourself." On a more galactic level, it is "I am everything, and everything is me." In this way, *In Lak'ech* transforms from the typical modern interpretation of how the ancient Maya would greet another person (by saying *In Lak'ech* instead of simply *hello*) into a sacred action of co-creation that is both a way to relate to other human beings and also with all other forms of life, with our planet, and with the entire cosmos in both the seen and unseen realms.

Applied to human relations, *In Lak'ech* is the reality that if I hurt you, I ultimately hurt myself; if I help you, I ultimately help myself. This is a wonderful view, and we can only imagine what life would be like on our planet if everyone would embrace its values. Taken one step further, *In Lak'ech* can also be applied when relating to the natural world. We can practice *In Lak'ech* with the trees and animals and oceans and clouds. In doing so, we not only honor the interconnectedness of all life, but we also begin to align our actions with all of creation.

That is why at the "biggest" level, *In Lak'ech* also unites us to a "galactic" awareness of our Luminous Self that the Maya and other cultures with this level of awareness embrace(d) as a way of life. One of my first true "awakenings" to this level of awareness occurred when I started to spend time with my Wirrarika mentors. When the Wirrarika go on the sacred pilgrimage to the peyote desert of Wirikuta to seek a vision for what to do with their lives, they dig up a special root from the ground to make a paint, which they then apply to both cheeks on their face in the shape of a galactic spiral. This is an action of acknowledgment of *In Lak'ech*—that the spirals on my fingertips and the spiraling shape of a seashell, a whirlpool, or a tornado are exactly the same as the spiraling shape of our galaxy or the mapping of our DNA. The practice of *In Lak'ech* connects us in the most sacred and intimate way with everything by acknowledging that there is no division between "me," "my consciousness," and all of creation.

Practice:
the art of counterpractice

Living through the Luminous Self could, in general, be described as living in a way almost completely counter to the way hypnotized people live now. The true practice of *In Lak'ech* oftentimes causes a major problem for us simply because it goes completely against the current structure of our competitive society based on economic growth. It goes against the very structure of the reality currently held by most of the people around us. This is why it is so essential that we begin to act differently from normal in order to awaken to the Luminous Self.

The art of counterpractice is a technique that teaches us how to do just that. It allows us to begin the process of independence from the hypnotized world by showing us that our habitual thoughts and actions are not the only way to think and act. The premise is quite simple, although in practice it may be one of the most challenging things we could ever attempt. In *Ecoshamanism,* I delve further into sharing techniques of counterpractice toward a more healthy relationship to the world in an ecological sense. But counterpractice can be applied at all levels of consciousness, and here I will be addressing counterpractice as it relates to human relationships and the awakening of the Luminous Self.

The process begins by simply asking yourself, "What would it be like if I acted (or reacted) counter to my usual way?" For example, if I am someone who does nice things for people all the time, what would it be like if I stopped that and let other people do nice things for me for a change? If I'm someone who normally is very talkative and is accustomed to dominating conversations, what would happen if I shut my mouth and listened to others instead? If I usually get upset about things, what would it feel like if I simply did not?

Asking ourselves these types of questions over and over, and then actually practicing the counter action, or reaction, to our normal ways always leads to the enlightenment that our familiar response to life isn't always the only way, or best way, or healthiest way.

Counterpractice is far from easy, because our deeply ingrained habits will scream in protest when we try and alter them. The dominating quality of the Western ego fears the idea of letting go of control and melding with something so vast as the consciousness of the Luminous Self. When we are hypnotized, we allow our perceptions to be swayed by the consensus of other people, and the consensus then determines the one reality in which we live.

But the Tibetan Tum-mo practitioner that comfortably sits naked in the freezing cold by activating the mystic fire or the modern physicist contemplating the multiple realities exhibited by Schrödinger's cat have little doubt that we create our own reality, and with counterpractice we enlarge the scope of possibility by transcending our limited, habitual patterns of thought and action.

Practice:
positive charging of the internal dialog

Our internal dialog, the voice within our mind—also referred to as self-talk and automatic thoughts—occurs repeatedly. These are perceptions from the events and situations that happen to us. This process occurs naturally in everyone, whether we are consciously or unconsciously aware of its presence. The important thing to realize about the internal dialog is that it is largely responsible for our actions. This makes it one of the most important items for living through the Luminous Self.

When our internal dialog is full of positive thoughts, we create an optimistic and constructive atmosphere that brings a brightness to our eyes; we feel energized and empowered. This attitude is broadcast through our body language and our voice.

Here are a few tips to charging the internal dialog with positive energy:

POSITIVE APPROACH: There's a big difference between a negative thought and the reality of whether a situation is truly negative. Sometimes even having a heart attack, or almost dying, can have a positive outcome. Some of the "worst" moments in my life have actually provided me with a greater sense of appreciation, humility, and strength. On a moment-to-moment basis, we keep a positive charge to our internal dialog by acknowledging that, in the bigger picture, we have the power to ultimately make positive any situation.

LEARNING EXPERIENCES: Every experience in life has the power to teach us something. When faced with challenging situations that could easily cause us to react frustrated or upset, it's a positive response to simply view these situations as learning experiences and not let them drag us into energy-draining emotions.

ACCEPTANCE AND CHANGE: Positive thinking is not about denying the "bad" things that are happening in our world. Just the opposite: truly positive thoughts require honesty, objectivity, and detachment. When our internal dialog is filled with these capacities, we then have the ability to make changes and not simply complain or deny.

POSITIVE STATEMENTS: Intentionally making positive statements to yourself and others can have a dramatic effect on your life (more about this in chapter 10).

VIGILANCE: Maintaining a positive dialog takes practice and vigilance. It's not easy to break habitual pessimistic thoughts and actions. Just trying to be optimistic all the time is not the solution, though, because that can be another form of denial. Vigilance in being honest about the entirety of situations is what keeps us authentically positive.

GOOD MEMORIES: Taking a positive approach, learning from challenging experiences, honestly accepting and changing "bad" circumstances, and being vigilant in our efforts naturally leads to positive outcomes, which then create "good" memories. The memory of positive internal dialog naturally helps maintain a positive dialog.

Positive and negative thinking are both contagious. Our internal dialog affects all the people we meet and interact with each day. Other people can instinctively, subconsciously, and physically sense what's going on in our inner dialog. This is why we choose to be around positive people once we have become positive ourselves. At the same time, we become much more tolerant in our thoughts toward those who are acting from negativity, and our honest positivity is then able to help spread authentic optimism that is seated in objectivity.

Chapter 10

The Power of Talking, Divining, and Healing Stones

"Grandmother, throughout my more than twenty-five years of learning shamanic techniques, I have gained the knowledge of working with many different kinds of energies and essences. Over the past few years, I have been drawn to the bones of my Mother, the incredible rock formations and stones that speak to me at various levels and in different ways. Feeling the effects of powerful places where the rock and stones are revealed as communicating entities has even led me to move my home to Sedona, Arizona, where the rocks are continuously drawing people from around the globe and delivering their messages. I have done much work in this sacred place, but I would like to learn more about the power of the stones and how they can help us during this great time of transformation we are living in. Can you help me to learn more and explain this to people?"

I am happy you have asked me about this, hijo. What you so casually refer to as "stones" are really complex energetic actions with traits and personalities that are much more varied and individualized than what you would think. Stones are amazing repositories of information and energy. They also have hidden capacities that can be used to collect and store energy, both at physical and psychic levels.

"I have felt very clearly what you are describing, Grandmother, but I'm trying to understand at a deeper level how this works."

It is important for you to remember that you are dealing with specific patterns of energy that are interacting, moving, and changing, even when they appear to your eyes as solid and dormant. You have to expand your perspective of what a stone actually is before you will be able to fully employ its powers. You are dealing here with things that are very old and that have very long memories. The red rocks here where you live—you know that they were formed about 230 million of your years ago, and that they traveled on the wind and water from hundreds of miles away. They have lived under the ocean. They have lived by the seashore and under the plains. Now they live in the free wind, under the sun and sky, as their journey continues. Every stone has its own unique story to tell. Do you realize the ancient energies and memories that you are dealing with?

"Thank you for reminding me, Grandmother. I always think of the rocks as being extremely old, but I sometimes forget that they are in motion, much the same as everything else around me, and that they have had such a wide variety of experiences."

When working together with stones, you must keep that awareness with you at all times. Remember that even though you don't see the growth or decay of a tree from moment to moment, that tree is evolving in every second. And just like a tree, a stone contains the energetic memory of its life. The memory of the stone includes how it was formed, where it has lived, the unique journey it has made. Here in Sedona you have the young black rocks that were formed from the lava that caps your mountains. You have the white rocks that were left by the ocean. Then there are the towering red rocks that used to be part of the ancestral Rocky Mountains and that have been turned a color that inspires the human mind. And you also have the elders that live in the bottom of the canyon that hold the memories of the great fault lines that slowly move across your Mother's body. So, hijo, you see that each rock has a different story. The challenge for you is to learn how to communicate more deeply with them.

"I have been working on that, and it seems that I become more open to communication when my energy is strong and clear—and also when I turn down my thoughts and turn up my inner light. Is there anything else you suggest I do?"

There are many things, hijo. But first of all you must get to know them, develop a relation-ship with them. I suggest you carry them with you for a while, at least the smaller ones; be aware of them throughout the day, let your energy field mingle with theirs. Then put them under your pillow at night, and let your unconscious mind relate to them. At first it might be better to do this one at a time so there will not be too many unfamiliar voices. Once you are familiar with them as individuals, you will be able to relate to them better as a group.

By personally interacting with each stone, you will be able to discern the type of gifts it may offer and what you might give in return.

"I understand that the composition and memory of a stone gives each one unique abilities. Some can be asked to help heal the physical body, others work more on the psyche, some are good for grounding during difficult times, while others work magic at helping to manifest intent. I'm sure these are some of the gifts you speak of. But what do we give back to the stones in return? I have made many hundreds of offerings to the sacred places and the Kakaiyeri, but never yet to a single stone."

It is much the same thing as you have been doing in your work with your sacred sites, hijo. You just feed the stone what it likes, take care of it, and listen to its wishes. You will know if you are doing the right thing, because you will feel the energy of the stone increasing or decreas-ing. To keep your stones energetically healthy, they need to eat, work, play, and rest. Some stones are reenergized by water, others like to be out in the sun or buried in the soil. The stones with the most powerful magic will at times ask for blood. The better you know the stones you work with, the easier it is to keep them happy.

Practice:
encountering a téka

We don't really have a name in our language for the special stones that we can work with and learn from. Many cultures, including the Wirrarika and Inca people whom I have lived with, do have names for these entities. Here I will borrow the Wirrarika name, *téka*.

Encountering a téka most often happens when you least expect it. Just like the old adage "a watched pot never boils," those that go "hunting" for a téka rarely find an authentic one. Although I have heard stories of people encountering a téka indoors in such places as malls and rock shops, the vast majority of encounters happen when you get yourself out into nature and listen for the téka singing. Listening for a singing stone may sound like a strange notion, but I assure you it is happening all around you once you are open to perceiving it.

Not all stones will be tékas for you, but all have the capacity. Think of it this way: not all the people you meet become your most important teachers, but each one of them could. That is the way to think about encountering a téka. It will be much easier to work with a téka that is put naturally in your path rather than to go searching especially for one—that is to say, if you are simply taking a walk in nature near your home, or have spent much time and energy to visit a special sacred site in a far-off land, always be aware of the chance to meet a téka, but it's better not to specifically go shopping for one, like you would a new pair of shoes. Synchronistic events almost always accompany the encounter with a téka.

Many people like to collect "special" stones that catch their eye or evoke a certain unique feeling. Like me, you probably know of someone who has piles or even bags of special stones they have collected. So how do you know when you encounter a téka? The answer is simple: you just know. When you encounter a téka, you will know. If you are not sure, then chances are you have not found one. They are that special.

Now that is not to say that you will immediately know what that téka is about, what its gifts are, if it would like to work with you, if it would like to be left alone, if it needs to be fed, etc. It may take a good long while before those things are revealed. I found a powerful téka lying on the side of the dirt road leading to my house just a few months ago. I knew to take this téka home with me, but I still haven't found out why. Maybe the téka simply wanted to come inside for a while. Even though I've been very busy and haven't tried very often to communicate with this téka, I am confident that when the time is right, we will have some very important conversations and we will learn much about each other. The point here is to not try to hurry things. Sometimes a téka will sing or speak to you immediately, and other times not. When the appropriate moment comes, you will know.

So once you encounter a téka, what then? Well, this is where intuition and experience comes in. Now, chances are you will make the correct decision as to what to do next, because when or if you ever encounter a téka, you can be sure it's no accident. The two of you have met for some reason. So take your time and evaluate the situation with all the resources you have.

For example, assess what your physical body is telling you about the téka. What impressions do you get with your eyes? If you feel it is safe to pick up the téka, how does it feel in your hands? Now what about your emotions? How do you feel about this téka? What does your inner knowing, or intuition, tell you?

At this point, it is good to make a small survey of the types of specialties involved with tékas:

- A téka that appeals to you visually, physically, and that feels somehow familiar to you may be a companion or guardian téka.
- Tékas that wear naturally formed designs or patterns should be looked at very carefully, for the symbolism of the markings may well be a physical manifestation of the téka's personality or job.
- Some tékas specialize in the ability to collect and then discharge luminous energy and are very useful in healing.
- There are also tékas that collect "shadow" energy and have the ability to cleanse this energy by releasing it into the earth.
- Dreaming tékas communicate best when your consciousness is steered away from purely human concerns, such as during times of intense ritual or during the different levels of sleep.
- Tékas that manifest in meaningful shapes, such as hearts, triangles, circles, etc., may have hidden secrets relevant to their physical form. Different shapes and textures inspire various responses, depending on the individual. Only you will know what the different forms will mean to you.
- Magical or manifesting tékas have the ability to help you concentrate and focus your intent. Many times, but not always, they physically appear as clear or shiny stones.

With these characteristics in mind, you may be able to determine, at least initially, your best course of action when first encountering a téka. Remember that there could be many reasons for your meeting. It could be that the téka has one important message

Some of my tékas recharging in the sun and "conversing" with one another. (Photo: Nancy Bartell)

for you, and that is all. If that is the case, it wouldn't be right to take the téka with you, because maybe that téka has a message for someone else that will come along to that same place. Just because you receive something from a téka doesn't mean you should remove it from where it currently lives.

On the other hand, you may be given the strong insight that the téka wishes to go with you. In this case, be open to the possibility that this may just be temporary. Maybe the téka has a job to do with you or someone else, or even many people or places, but then will wish to return to where it was living. No matter what, in properly honoring a téka, you must be open to what it wants, and it may want to return either periodically or permanently to where you two originally met.

There are also occasions where you will meet a téka that will be a life-long companion, friend, colleague, teacher, or assistant. Some cultures even pass tékas from one generation of shaman to the next, and in this way the tékas become part of the family for many generations. This is not surprising, as a true encounter between a person and a téka is an extremely powerful metaphysical occurrence that is outside the realm of human control. My Wirrarika mentors even have tékas in which the life-force of a person is charged, so when the person has died from their body, the tiny (normally pea-sized) but powerful téka is kept in a ceremonial bundle by the family and then fed during special holidays and fiestas. In this way, the spirit of the ancestors continues to live with and support the family and tribe.

Practice:
working with and caring for a téka

In all cases when you encounter a téka, there will be an exchange of energy. Even if you simply receive something from the téka such as a message, a feeling, a vision, and then shortly thereafter move on and never see the téka again, it is still always appropriate to give something to the téka in return. Depending on what happened between you and the téka, this could take countless forms.

Sometimes it is enough to simply say a heartfelt thanks. Other times, the téka may ask you for something. It could be a hug, it could be a bath, it could be a ride in your car. Many times a téka that does not wish to be removed from its place will ask you to bring someone else, or maybe many people, to visit and receive messages, insights, or healing.

But when you encounter a téka that will be living with you, your care and reciprocity with the téka will be much different. In all cases, no matter what your relationship with a particular téka, the téka will have a job or task that it is performing. In return for services provided, you will be required to nourish and care for the téka. Because these two topics (working with and caring for the téka) are so interconnected, I will deal with them together. These may include but are not limited to:

GUARDIAN TÉKA: The task of this téka is what its name implies. In some cases, it is like a bodyguard that you keep with you for safety. Tékas of this specialty often have the ability to intuitively warn you and/or give advice during the course of your day. Other types of guardian tékas include those that look after your house and are often kept on a front porch or inside, on a mantle or altar. Garden guardians keep safe the living plants and soil, and I have even met guardian tékas that keep pets safe and are often kept in or underneath their beds. As compared with other types of tékas that expend more energy, guardian tékas typically require only periodic feedings of thanks and prayers of gratefulness from you. That is what they primarily feed on. They like to be told they are doing a good job and to know that they are appreciated. If at times they ask for something more, be sure to respond accordingly.

LUMINOUS TÉKA: If you have a relationship with one of these tékas, you are truly fortunate. They are the Light Workers of the Kakaiyeri, and as such are natural healers. Basically what they do is collect luminous energy from sources such as the sun, fire, water, soil, wind, pollen, juice, blood, liqueur, sap, or saliva, among others, and then transfer the energy of that life-force to another living being, place, or space. If you or someone else requires an infusion of energy, this téka can help provide it. Especially when doing healing work, oftentimes the person (or other being) can't be taken to a place where they can receive a direct energetic infusion from, for example, a sacred spring or fire or mountaintop. In this case, the luminous téka can be taken to the place, infused with energy, and then used by the healer to impart the luminous energy from the téka (or used by the individual themselves to receive the energy). Unless you have been trained by someone who knows how to do this, it is wise to first familiarize yourself with this process by working with it on yourself. Feed the téka with one source of luminous energy at a time. For example, feed the téka the light, heat, and flowing mystical properties of fire, and then sometime later or the next day when you are not with the fire any longer, ask the téka to release the fire energy into your total human organism—mind/body/environment/spirit—and learn firsthand the effects of that infusion. Then afterwards listen to the téka for what it needs. Many times when working with fire, the téka will then want water or some other form of liquid. Once you have worked with the téka during many different types of infusions, you will likely find the téka has more ability to transfer certain energies than others. It's common for some tékas to work better with fire and sun, while others have keener talents for water or soil.

SHADOW TÉKA: I have noticed that many people involved in personal growth and spiritual awakening tend to focus on "enlightenment" by emphasizing "being in the light" and positive thoughts, prayers, and intentions. This is wonderful. However, negative thoughts and emotions, sickness, and darkness are just as much a part of our world right now, and they can't simply be ignored. Shadow tékas have the ability to help us deal in a positive way with these shadow aspects of life. The best way I have found to work with a shadow téka is to bury the téka in the ground at least overnight. In this way, the téka is cleansed by the enormous capacity of our Mother to absorb and heal shadow energy. Then the téka can be taken to calm anger, pull out sickness, absorb depression, and generally help to restore balance between light and dark when the shadow has taken over. Many techniques exist for working with a shadow téka. Some include placing the téka onto each chakra area of a "patient" while making prayers of intention, placing the téka in a special little "necklace bag" that is worn for a full day and night, sleeping with the téka under your pillow, ritually confessing your energetic "drains" to the téka, and taking the téka with you into the tomb during the embrace of the earth ceremony,[17] among others. Once the téka has drawn the shadow energy into its body, the téka must be cleansed by either burying it in the soil overnight or placing it next to a very hot fire until it is hot and then into the youngest spring water available.

DREAMING TÉKA: During periods of altered states of consciousness, a dreaming téka can help to focus the often random perceptions, images, and messages that we are accessing. I have employed the help of a dreaming téka by simply holding the téka in my hands while speaking with Grandfather Fire, by placing the téka on the ground in front of me while sitting in meditation, by having the téka with me during the sweat lodge ceremony and also while questing for vision on the land,[18] and of course by having the téka next to me on my nightstand or under my pillow while sleeping. I have found that dreaming tékas like to be fed and cared for in unusual ways. My dreaming téka has asked to be attached to my dog's collar when we go hiking; likes to watch educational programs on TV and listen to music; asks to sit in various places in nature, especially nearby Oak Creek, for periods of time up to a full week; and likes to be placed and held in my mouth and the mouths of others (after being washed, of course), among others.

MAGICAL TÉKA: While all tékas have their own special sort of "magic," there are some tékas that are extremely "fluid," adaptable, spontaneous in action, unpredictable although very disciplined, and that inspire you to fulfill tasks and dreams. These are the tékas I refer to as magical or manifesting tékas, and although they can be very helpful, you must be careful with them because you never know what will happen when you work with them. A magical téka does not care much about what you think of yourself or what you are doing with your life. A magical téka will show you who you really are and what to do in order to flow with creation, and many times this will be very different than what you expect. Magical tékas are also known for "coyote teaching," which is very tricky. For example, if you employ a magical téka to

17 See *Ecoshamanism*, page 181.
18 See *Ecoshamanism*, page 215.

help you learn how to heal people that have pain in their body, the magical téka may send you pain as a way of teaching you how to deal with it.

HAPPY TÉKA: I only just recently discovered what I can only describe as happy, or joyful, tékas. These tékas are often found in groups. They have a similar feeling as the luminous tékas, but the difference is that unlike the true luminous téka that likes and even needs to "work," the happy tékas accomplish their task by simply making you feel happy.

Practice:
sacred sites

It is quite common to encounter tékas at both natural and humanmade sacred sites. Sometimes the site is considered sacred for the very reason that the tékas abide there. For example, the rock in the center of the Dome of the Rock is one of the holiest sites in the world to Muslims, Jews, and Christians. Muslims believe the rock to be the spot from which Muhammad ascended to God in heaven, accompanied by the angel Gabriel. For Jews, the stone is the site where Abraham fulfilled God's test to see if he would be willing to sacrifice his son Isaac. Aside from Christian beliefs that Jesus used the temple, many also believe that the tomb under the temple was the place where Jesus was buried and then resurrected.

In most cases, tékas at sacred sites will not want to leave, and you should not attempt to take them away with you. They have a job to perform with the people that come to the sacred site, and if we take them away we do a disservice to those that come after us.

However, many times we make a great effort to travel to a sacred site, even to a far-away country, so it is very tempting and quite normal to desire to bring something from the site home with you as a memory of the unique qualities and energy of the site. Collecting a stone or two from the sacred site may seem like an innocent way to do this. But we have to ask ourselves: *What if everyone did it?* Out of respect and reciprocity with the site, we have an obligation to protect it. Having dealt with this situation for many years, I would like to offer an effective alternative.

Sacred rock for Christians, Muslims, and Jews. (Photo:
American Colony, Jerusalem, 1933)

I have found that with a little effort and help received from the tékas, we can bring the essence and energy of a sacred site home with us without actually taking anything physical from the site. This is done by infusing the energy of the sacred site into a "blank," or empty, stone that you bring with you from home and take back home with you once the stone is infused with the energy of the sacred site. In this way, the stone becomes a téka of the sacred site. The process goes like this:

1. Acquire a piece of clear or semi-transparent stone the size of a pea up to the size of your fist. Quartz and amethyst are good choices. Also acquire a piece of cloth of an appropriate size to wrap up the stone.

2. Next, purify the stone by bathing it in spring water. Placing the stone in water from a natural spring where, or close to where, the water comes from the earth is best. In a pinch, you can use bottled spring water, but try to use water that comes from a glass container, not plastic.

3. Now bathe the cloth in the same water and immediately wrap the stone in the cloth. You can wring the cloth out first so it isn't totally soaked. The important thing is that they are both purified with the "young" water. (I have been told that wrapping the stone in tin foil works also, but I don't like the idea and have had sufficiently good results using a cloth.)

4. When you arrive with your stone at the sacred site, it is completely up to you how you go about infusing the stone and how much time you will have. If possible, try to have the stone spend a whole day and night. But even if you are only there a few hours, that can often be enough. In all cases, speak to the beings, energies, and essences of the site, both seen and unseen, about what you are doing, and respectfully request for your stone to be infused with the power of the site before placing it on or in the ground, in a tree, etc.

5. Once your stone has been infused with the unique qualities and wisdom of the site, you will now be able to invoke not only the memories of the place that you keep in your personal organism but also what has been stored in the stone.

I have found this technique to be very useful in the protection of sacred sites, and it really does work to help you bring home the energy of the site without physically affecting the site.

Working with the tékas is a profoundly proactive way of aligning with creation. With patience and practice, learning to work with the tékas can truly be an unlimited source of wisdom and inspiration as we move toward healing and awakening our connection to the divine.

Living with Earth Changes: Advice from Elders, Scientists, and Community Leaders

Many people have awakened to the need to change the way we are stewarding our beautiful planet. We need to start right now. The messages from the First Shamans, as well as those awakened people that understand and are taking action, can broadly be boiled down to four main categories:

1. That the planet we live on, our miraculous Mother Earth, is a living and breathing entity that needs to be protected from the mindless greed and exploitation of the human race. It is time that we wake up and develop healthy and harmonious ways of living in a sustainable fashion with the planet that provides us with life.

2. That the peoples of the world need to unite for the common good and humanity mature so that race, nationality, and religious affiliations don't stand in the way of conducting human affairs in a healthy and peaceful manner.

3. That compassion, caring, charity, and love replace hatred and bigotry as we move forward in this time of great transformation and into a new age of global awareness and stewardship of our planet.

4. That education of the interconnection of all life be the cornerstone of social, political, and religious institutions that make up the human enterprise.

In terms of action, the transformation of consciousness toward conscious co-creation requires us to act in a more evolved manner. A list of some of these requirements might look like this:

- Require that our government treat all peoples with peace and compassion.
- Require our government not to grant more rights to corporations than it grants to individuals. People must be held accountable for their actions and not be allowed to hide behind their corporate "entities."
- Require our businesses to produce goods and services in a way that is not detrimental to the health of our biosphere.
- Require our media to provide honest information not dependent on commercialism but geared toward making informed decisions on both local and global situations and events.
- Require ourselves to actively help others to live through the Luminous Self and to encourage children, from an early age, to evolve spiritually through teaching about the interconnectedness of all life.
- Require ourselves to work "jobs" that serve to protect, preserve, and restore the delicate ecosystems of our planet, and develop new technologies that will enable us to live more harmoniously with the natural environments that sustain us.

These times of great challenges require us to stay focused and positive. When we believe we can do something, our rate of success is much greater than when we enter into something expecting not to be able to accomplish it. The power of positive statements is amazing, and the amount of past and present wisdom shared by them truly can be inspiring. There have been so many incredible people throughout history that have spoken wise and inspiring words that we can gain strength from in these times of change. I am also encouraged by how many of our current leaders and researchers are approaching the challenges facing humanity. Here are a few statements that I feel are very timely and important to reflect on:

The more we turn away from the instructions of the Great Spirit, the more signs we see in the form of earthquakes, floods, drought, fires, tornadoes, as Nature makes ready her revenge. All of this will happen at one time along with the wars and corruption. We see this now as young children become angry, killing each other and their parents. They show no respect. We are all corrupt. If this Purification does not materialize, then the world will turn over four times and will leave only ants here to start a new life. Before people came to this world they were sick, just as today we are sick from all this corruption. Now we are seeking a way to solve our present situation. This is the last world, we are not going anywhere from here. If we destroy this, the highest world, we will be given no other chances.

Let us consider this matter seriously so that this world is not destroyed, so that we can continue to live and save this land and life for the generations to come.

—*Delivered and submitted by Martin Gashweseoma, caretaker of the sovereign Hopi Nation, to the U.N. General Assembly, November 22, 1993*

We are now faced with great problems, not only here but throughout the land. Ancient cultures are being annihilated. Our peoples' lands are being taken from them, leaving them no place to call their own.

Why is this happening?

It is happening because many have given up or manipulated their original spiritual teachings. The way of life which the Great Spirit has given to all its people of the world, whatever your original instructions, are not being honored. It is because of this great sickness called greed, which infects every land and country, that simple people are losing what they have kept for thousands of years.

Now we are at the very end of our trail.

Many people no longer recognize the true path of the Great Spirit. They have, in fact, no respect for the Great Spirit or for our precious Mother Earth, who gives us all life. We are instructed in our ancient prophecy that this would occur . . . .

All over the world there are now many signs that nature is no longer in balance. Floods, drought, earthquakes, and great storms are occurring and causing much suffering. We do not want this to occur in our country and we pray to the

Great Spirit to save us from such things. But there are now signs that this very same thing might happen very soon on our own land.

Now we must look upon each other as brothers and sisters. There is no more time for divisions between people. Today I call upon all of us, from right here at home, Hotevilla, where we too are guilty of gossiping and causing divisions even among our own families, out to the entire world where thievery, war, and lying go on every day. These divisions will not be our salvation. Wars only bring more wars, never peace.

Only by joining together in a Spiritual Peace with love in our hearts for one another, love in our hearts for the Great Spirit and Mother Earth, shall we be saved from the terrible Purification Day which is just ahead…

God bless you, each one of you, and know our prayers for peace meet yours as the sun rises and sets. May the Great Spirit guide you safely into the path of love, peace, freedom, and God on this Earth Mother. May the holy ancestors of love and light keep you safe in your land and homes. Pray for God to give you something important to do in this great work which lies ahead of us all to bring peace on earth…

Be well, my children, and think good thoughts of peace and togetherness. Peace for all life on earth and peace with one another in our homes, families, and countries. We are not so different in the Creator's eyes. The same great Father Sun shines his love on each of us daily just as Mother Earth prepares the sustenance for our table, do they not?

We are one after all.

—Dan Evehema, Hopi Eldest Elder, "His Final Message to Mankind,"
From Hotevilla, Arizona, 1996 (http://www.hopiland.net/prophecy/dan-1.htm)

Native American Code of Ethics:

1. Each morning upon rising, and each evening before sleeping, give thanks for the life within you and for all life, for the good things the Creator has given you and for the opportunity to grow a little more each day. Consider your thoughts and actions of the past day and seek for the courage and strength to be a better person. Seek for the things that will benefit others (everyone).

2. Respect. Respect means "to feel or show honor or esteem for someone or something; to consider the well-being of, or to treat someone or something with deference or courtesy." Showing respect is a basic law of life.

a. Treat every person, from the tiniest child to the oldest elder, with respect at all times.

b. Special respect should be given to elders, parents, teachers, and community leaders.

c. No person should be made to feel "put down" by you; avoid hurting other hearts as you would avoid a deadly poison.

d. Touch nothing that belongs to someone else (especially sacred objects) without permission or an understanding between you.

e. Respect the privacy of every person; never intrude on a person's quiet moment or personal space.

f. Never walk between people that are conversing.

g. Never interrupt people who are conversing.

h. Speak in a soft voice, especially when you are in the presence of elders, strangers, or others to whom special respect is due.

i. Do not speak unless invited to do so at gatherings where elders are present (except to ask what is expected of you, should you be in doubt).

j. Never speak about others in a negative way, whether they are present or not.

k. Treat the earth and all of her aspects as your Mother. Show deep respect for the mineral world, the plant world, and the animal world. Do nothing to pollute our Mother; rise up with wisdom to defend her.

l. Show deep respect for the beliefs and religion of others.

m. Listen with courtesy to what others say, even if you feel that what they are saying is worthless. Listen with your heart.

n. Respect the wisdom of the people in council. Once you give an idea to a council meeting, it no longer belongs to you. It belongs to the people. Respect demands that you listen intently to the ideas of others in council and that you do not insist that your idea prevail. Indeed, you should freely support the ideas of others if they are true and good, even if those ideas are quite different from the ones you have contributed. The clash of ideas brings forth the spark of truth.

3. Once a council has decided something in unity, respect demands that no one speak secretly against what has been decided. If the council has made an error, that error will become apparent to everyone in its own time.

4. Be truthful at all times and under all conditions.

5. Always treat your guests with honor and consideration. Give of your best food, your best blankets, the best part of your house, and your best service to your guests.

chapter 11

6. The hurt of one is the hurt of all; the honor of one is the honor of all.
7. Receive strangers and outsiders with a loving heart and as members of the human family.
8. All the races and tribes in the world are like the different-colored flowers of one meadow. All are beautiful. As children of the Creator, they must all be respected.
9. To serve others, to be of some use to family, community, nation, and the world is one of the main purposes for which human beings have been created. Do not fill yourself with your own affairs and forget your most important talks. True happiness comes only to those who dedicate their lives to the service of others.
10. Observe moderation and balance in all things.
11. Know those things that lead to your well-being and those things that lead to your destruction.
12. Listen to and follow the guidance given to your heart. Expect guidance to come in many forms; in prayer, in dreams, in times of quiet solitude, and in the words and deeds of wise elders and friends.

—Courtesy of Four Worlds Institute.
Originally published in the book
The Sacred Tree (*http://www.4worlds.org/*)

The most important human endeavor is the striving for morality in our actions. Our inner balance, and even our very existence depends on it. Only morality in our actions can give beauty and dignity to our lives.

—Albert Einstein

Man must evolve for all human conflict a method which rejects revenge, aggression and retaliation. The foundation of such a method is love.

—Martin Luther King

The breeze at dawn has secrets to tell you.
Don't go back to sleep.
You must ask for what you really want.
Don't go back to sleep.
People are going back and forth across the doorsill where two worlds touch.
The round door is open.
Don't go back to sleep.

—Rumi

If you want others to be happy, practice compassion. If you want to be happy, practice compassion.

—*The Dalai Lama*

We must be the change we wish to see in the world.

—*Gandhi*

Never doubt that a small group of thoughtful, committed citizens can change the world. Indeed, it is the only thing that ever has.

—*Margaret Mead*

We must not, in trying to think about how we can make a big difference, ignore the small daily differences we can make which, over time, add up to big differences that we often cannot foresee.

—*Marian Wright-Edelman*

How wonderful it is that nobody need wait a single minute before starting to improve the world.

—*Anne Frank*

The important thing is this: to be able at any moment to sacrifice what we are for what we could become.

—*Charles DuBois*

The trouble with the rat race is that even if you win you're still a rat.

—*Lily Tomlin*

People are always blaming their circumstances for what they are. I don't believe in circumstances. The people who get on in this world are the people who get up and look for the circumstances they want, and, if they can't find them, make them.

—*George Bernard Shaw*

chapter 11

Practice:
the power of positive statements

The competency to effect positive change begins with what we say to ourselves and everything around us. Intentionally practicing positive statements in a variety of situations helps to manifest positive outcomes. Once we awaken to aspects of living in conscious co-creation, positive statements then serve to reinforce our relationships and give strength in meeting challenges. For example, in the intentional practice of *In Lak'ech* (chapter 9), we focus on the fact that we are essentially a part of, or the same as, everything around us. Following this, if we should happen to be in a situation where someone was yelling at us as a result of their own inner conflict, we could use the power of the positive statement and repeating to ourselves while looking at that person, "You are my other self, you are my other self," and in this way using your calmness and compassion to help alleviate anger.

This can also be applied when connecting with nature. For example, if you are in the presence of a large and beautiful tree, while hugging the tree you use the positive statement and connect at a deeper level. For example, I say, "Hugging this tree, I feel the power and strength of life. I give thanks to be here in this moment." The same can be done while sitting on the shore of a lake or while walking in the sunshine. Some of my favorite positive statements include:

1. "I am guided through my day to do good in the world,
   for I am in alignment with creation."
2. "I bring peace to the world, for I am at peace with myself."
3. "I shall do no evil, for I am conscious of what I create."
4. "I have abundant energy, for I am intentionally connected to the Source."
5. "I am connected to the sacred fire, for I am a little sun walking the earth."
6. "I give love and support, and therefore I am surrounded by love and support."
7. "I can do it!"
8. "I attract abundance, for I am truly thankful for the abundance in my life."
9. "There are only situations, not problems."
10. "I am my Luminous Self."

Sometimes our light goes out but is blown into a flame by another human being. Each of us owes deepest thanks to those who have rekindled this light.

—*Albert Schweitzer*

Do your little bit of good where you are; it's those little bits of good put together that overwhelm the world.

—*Archbishop Desmond Tutu*

In the midst of global crises such as pollution, wars, and famine, kindness may too easily be dismissed as a "soft issue" or a luxury to be addressed after the urgent problems are solved. But kindness is the greatest need in all those areas —kindness toward the environment, toward other nations, toward the needs of people who are suffering. Until we reflect basic kindness in everything we do, our political gestures will be fleeting and fragile. Simple kindness may be the most vital key to the riddle of how human beings can live with each other in peace and care properly for this planet we all share.

—*Bo Lozoff*

If you light a lamp for somebody, it will also brighten your path.

—*Buddhist saying*

Human Creations: Can We Evolve Toward Conscious Co-creation?

In conclusion, I would like to acknowledge the amazing capacity of human beings to create. We have come so far in so little time. With all of the astonishing creations we have manifested onto the earth, the question now is whether we can evolve from creating things that purely serve humanity into conscious co-creation with our organic home. The following appendix of the chronology of human advancement clearly demonstrates the creative potential of our species. It is my hope and prayer that we can transform this potential in order to save ourselves before it's too late. With each one of us doing our part to live through the Luminous Self, we can awaken the world and transform human consciousness. That is the positive message of hope delivered by the First Shamans.

We can do it!

CHRONOLOGY OF HUMAN ADVANCEMENT

NOTE: Some dates, places, and people listed here may be debatable. This information is presented only as a general overview, and although compiled by many reputable sources, it may contain inaccuracies.

Paleolithic Era

- Indeterminate: Language
- 2.4 mya: Olduwan—struck-stone tools in East Africa
- 1.8 mya: *Homo erectus* appears
- 1.65 mya: Acheulean—struck and reworked stone tools in Kenya
- 1 mya: Controlled fire and cooking in East Africa
- 500 tya: Shelter construction
- 130 tya: *Homo sapiens* (modern humans) appear
- 100–500 tya: Clothing
- 400 tya: Pigments in Zambia
- 400 tya: Spears in Germany
- 100 tya: Lithic blades in Africa and the Near East

- 60 tya: Ships probably used by settlers of New Guinea
- 50 tya: Flute in Slovenia
- 50 tya: Bow in Tunisia
- 43 tya: Mining in Swaziland and Hungary
- 37 tya: Tally sticks in Swaziland
- 30 tya: Sewing needles
- 26 tya: Ceramics in Moravia
- 12 tya: Pottery in Japan

tenth millennium BC

- Agriculture and alcoholic beverages in the Fertile Crescent
- Adobe in the Near East
- 9500 BC: Granary (grain storehouse) in the Jordan Valley

ninth millennium BC

- 8700 BC: Metalworking (copper pendant) in Iraq

eighth millennium BC

- Animal husbandry in the Near East
- Plaster in Jericho

seventh millennium BC

- Cloth woven from flax fiber

sixth millennium BC

- Irrigation in the Fertile Crescent
- Ploughs in Mesopotamia

fifth millennium BC

- Beer and bread in Sumer
- Wheel and axle combination in Mesopotamia

fourth millennium BC

- 4000 BC: Canal in Mesopotamia
- 3800 BC: Engineered roadway in England
- 3500 BC: Plywood in Egypt
- 3500 BC: Writing in Sumer
- 3500 BC: Carts in Sumer
- 3100 BC: Drainage in the Indus Valley Civilization (India/Pakistan)
- Dental surgery in Mehrgarh (Indus Valley Civilization)
- Bronze: Susa
- Silk in China
- Cement in Egypt
- River boats in Egypt

third millennium BC

- 2800 BC: Soap in Mesopotamia
- 2800 BC: Egyptians devise the 12-month, 365-day calendar
- 2800 BC: Button in the Indus Valley Civilization
- 2600 BC: Artificial sewage systems in the Indus Valley Civilization
- 2500 BC: Flush toilets in the Indus Valley Civilization
- 2400 BC: Shipyard in Lothal (Indus Valley Civilization)
- 2000 BC: Currency
- Sledges in Scandinavia
- Alphabet in Egypt
- Candles in Egypt
- Abacus in China

second millennium BC

- Glass in Egypt
- Earliest medical textbook

- Rubber in Mesoamerica
- Spoked-wheel chariot in the Near East
- Water clock in Egypt
- Bells in China

first millennium BC

- 600s BC: Coins in Lydia
- 500s BC: Sugar in India
- 500s BC: Dental bridge in Etruria
- 500s BC: Trebuchet in China
- 400 BC: Greeks invent the catapult, the first military weapon
- 300s BC: Compass in China
- 300s BC: Screw: Archytas
- 200s BC: Crossbow in China
- 200s BC: Compound pulley: Archimedes
- 150s BC: Clockwork (the Antikythera mechanism)
- 150s BC: Astrolabe: Hipparchus
- 100s BC: Parchment in Pergamon
- 1st century BC: Glassblowing in Syria
- 40 BC: earliest known rolling-element bearing in Roman ship

first millennium

- 50: Mouldboard plough in Gaul
- 100s: Aeolipile: Hero of Alexandria
- 100s: Stern-mounted rudder in China
- 105: Paper invented in China
- 200s: Wheelbarrow: Zhuge Liang
- 200s: Horseshoes in Germany
- 300: Wootz steel in India

- 300s: Stirrup in China
- 300s: Toothpaste in Egypt
- 400s Horse collar in China
- 600s: Windmill in Persia
- 600s: The heavy plow by the Slavs
- 673: Greek fire: Kallinikos of Heliopolis
- 700: Quill pen
- 700s: Horseshoes in Europe
- 800s: Gunpowder in China
- 852: Parachute: Armen Firman
- Woodblock printing in China
- Porcelain in China
- Spinning wheel in China or India

second millennium, eleventh century

- 1041: Movable type printing press: Bi Sheng

twelfth century

- 1100: Water power used in iron making in Europe
- 1128: Cannon in China
- 1180: Windmills in Europe

thirteenth century

- 1280s: Eyeglasses in northern Italy
- Sandpaper in China

fourteenth century

- Mechanical clocks in northern Italy
- 1350: Suspension bridges in Peru

fifteenth century

- Arquebus and rifle in Europe
- 1441: Rain gauge: Jang Yeong-sil
- 1450s: Alphabetic, movable type printing press: Johann Gutenberg
- 1451: Concave lens for eyeglasses: Nicholas of Cusa
- 1490–1492: Nürnberg Terrestrial Globe: Martin Behaim
- 1498: Toothbrush in China

sixteenth century

- 1500 (circa): Ball bearing: Leonardo Da Vinci
- 1500 (circa): Scissors: Leonardo Da Vinci
- 1503: Mona Lisa portrait: Leonardo Da Vinci
- 1510: Pocket watch: Peter Henlein
- 1540: Ether: Valerius Cordus
- 1576: Ironclad warship: Oda Nobunaga
- 1581: Pendulum: Galileo Galilei
- 1582: Gregorian calendar: multiple inventors
- 1589: Stocking frame: William Lee
- 1593: Thermometer: Galileo Galilei
- Musket in Europe
- Pencil in England

seventeenth century

- 1608: Telescope: Hans Lippershey
- 1609: Microscope: Galileo Galilei
- 1620: Slide rule: William Oughtred
- 1631: Vernier scale: Pierre Vernier
- 1642: Adding machine: Blaise Pascal
- 1643: Barometer: Evangelista Torricelli

- 1645: Vacuum pump: Otto von Guericke
- 1657: Pendulum clock: Christiaan Huygens
- 1672: Steam car: Ferdinand Verbiest
- 1679: Pressure cooker: Denis Papin
- 1698: Steam engine: Thomas Savery
- 1700: Piano: Bartolomeo Cristofori

eighteenth century

- 1701: Seed drill: Jethro Tull
- 1709: Iron smelting using coke: Abraham Darby I
- 1712: Steam piston engine: Thomas Newcomen
- 1710: Thermometer: René Antoine Ferchault de Réaumur
- 1711: Tuning fork: John Shore
- 1714: Mercury thermometer: Daniel Gabriel Fahrenheit
- 1730: Mariner's quadrant: Thomas Godfrey
- 1731: Sextant: John Hadley
- 1733: Flying shuttle: John Kay
- 1742: Franklin stove: Benjamin Franklin
- 1750: Flatboat: Jacob Yoder
- 1752: Lightning rod: Benjamin Franklin
- 1764: Spinning jenny: James Hargreaves and Thomas Highs
- 1767: Carbonated water: Joseph Priestley
- 1769: Steam engine: James Watt
- 1769: Water frame: Richard Arkwright and Thomas Highs
- 1769: Steam car: Nicolas Cugnot
- 1775: Submarine Turtle: David Bushnell
- 1775: New kind of boring machine: John Wilkinson
- 1776: Steamboat: Claude de Jouffroy
- 1777: Card teeth making machine: Oliver Evans

- 1777: Circular saw: Samuel Miller
- 1779: Spinning mule: Samuel Crompton
- 1780s: Iron rocket: Tipu Sultan in India
- 1783: Multitubular boiler engine: John Stevens
- 1783: Parachute: Jean Pierre Blanchard
- 1783: Hot air balloon: Montgolfier brothers
- 1784: Bifocal glasses: Benjamin Franklin
- 1784: Argand lamp: Ami Argand
- 1784: Shrapnel shell: Henry Shrapnel
- 1785: Power loom: Edmund Cartwright
- 1785: Automatic flour mill: Oliver Evans
- 1786: Threshing machine: Andrew Meikle
- 1787: Non-condensing high pressure engine: Oliver Evans
- 1790: Cut and head nail machine: Jacob Perkins
- 1791: Artificial teeth: Nicholas Dubois De Chemant
- 1793: Cotton gin: Eli Whitney
- 1793: Optical telegraph: Claude Chappe
- 1797: Cast-iron plow: Charles Newbold
- 1798: Vaccination: Edward Jenner
- 1798: Lithography: Alois Senefelder
- 1799: Seeding machine: Eliakim Spooner

nineteenth century

THE 1800S

- 1800: Electric battery: Alessandro Volta
- 1801: Jacquard loom: Joseph Marie Jacquard
- 1802: Screw propeller steamboat Phoenix: John Stevens
- 1802: Gas stove: Zachäus Andreas Winzler
- 1804: Locomotive: Richard Trevithick

- 1805: Submarine Nautilus: Robert Fulton
- 1807: Steamboat Clermont: Robert Fulton
- 1808: Band saw: William Newberry
- 1809: Arc lamp: Humphry Davy

THE 1810S
- 1811: Gun breechloader: Thornton
- 1812: Metronome: Dietrich Nikolaus Winkel
- 1816: Miner's safety lamp: Humphry Davy
- 1816: Metronome: Johann Nepomuk Maelzel
- 1816: Stirling engine: Robert Stirling
- 1816: Stethoscope: Rene Theophile Hyacinthe Laennec
- 1817: Draisine or velocipede (two-wheeled): Karl Drais
- 1817: Kaleidoscope: David Brewster
- 1819: Breech loading flintlock: John Hall

THE 1820S
- 1821: Electric motor: Michael Faraday
- 1823: Electromagnet: William Sturgeon
- 1826: Photography: Joseph Nicéphore Niépce
- 1826: Internal combustion engine: Samuel Morey
- 1827: Insulated wire: Joseph Henry
- 1827: Screw propeller: Josef Ressel
- 1827: Friction match: John Walker

THE 1830S
- 1830: Lawn mower: Edwin Beard Budding
- 1830: Stenotype on punched paper strip: Karl Drais
- 1831: Multiple coil magnet: Joseph Henry
- 1831: Magnetic acoustic telegraph: Joseph Henry (patented 1837)
- 1831: Reaper: Cyrus McCormick

- 1831: Electrical generator: Michael Faraday and Ányos Jedlik
- 1834: The Hansom cab is patented
- 1834: Louis Braille perfects his Braille system
- 1834: Refrigerator: Jacob Perkins
- 1834: Combine harvester: Hiram Moore
- 1835: Photogenic drawing: William Henry Fox Talbot
- 1835: Revolver: Samuel Colt
- 1835: Morse code: Samuel Morse
- 1835: Electromechanical relay: Joseph Henry
- 1835: Incandescent light bulb: James Bowman Lindsay
- 1836: Samuel Colt receives a patent for the Colt revolver
- 1836: Improved screw propeller: John Ericsson
- 1836: Sewing machine: Josef Madersberger
- 1837: Photography: Louis-Jacques-Mandé Daguerre
- 1837: Steel plow: John Deere
- 1837: Camera Zoom Lens: Jozef Maximilián Petzval
- 1838: Electric telegraph: Charles Wheatstone (also Samuel Morse)
- 1838: Closed diving suit with a helmet: Augustus Siebe
- 1839: Vulcanization of rubber: Charles Goodyear

THE 1840S

- 1840: Screw-propelled frigate
- 1840: Artificial fertilizer: Justus von Liebig
- 1842: Anaesthesia: Crawford Long
- 1843: Typewriter: Charles Thurber
- 1843: Fax machine: Alexander Bain
- 1843: Ice cream maker: Nancy Johnson
- 1845: Portland cement: William Aspdin
- 1845: Double-tube tire: Robert Thomson

- 1846: Sewing machine: Elias Howe
- 1846: Rotary printing press: Richard M. Hoe
- 1849: Safety pin: Walter Hunt
- 1849: Francis turbine: James B. Francis
- 1849: Telephone: Antonio Meucci

THE 1850s

- 1852: Airship: Henri Giffard
- 1852: Passenger elevator: Elisha Otis
- 1852: Gyroscope: Léon Foucault
- 1853: Potato chips
- 1852: Paper bag: Francis Wolle
- 1855: Bunsen burner: Robert Bunsen
- 1858: Undersea telegraph cable: Fredrick Newton Gisborne
- 1858: Shoe sole sewing machine: Lyman R. Blake
- 1858: Mason jar: John L. Mason
- 1858: Can opener: Ezra Warner
- 1859: Oil drill: Edwin L. Drake

THE 1860s

- 1860: Linoleum: Fredrick Walton
- 1860: Repeating rifle: Oliver F. Winchester, Christopher Spencer
- 1860: Self-propelled torpedo: Giovanni Luppis
- 1860: Vacuum Cleaner: Daniel Hess
- 1861: Ironclad USS Monitor: John Ericsson
- 1861: Siemens regenerative furnace: Carl Wilhelm Siemens
- 1862: Revolving machine gun: Richard J. Gatling
- 1862: Pasteurization: Louis Pasteur, Claude Bernard
- 1863: Player piano: Henri Fourneaux
- 1864: First concept typewriter: Peter Mitterhofer

- 1865: Compression ice machine: Thaddeus Lowe
- 1865: Roller coaster: LaMarcus Adna Thompson
- 1865: Barbed wire: Louis Jannin
- 1866: Dynamite: Alfred Nobel
- 1868: First practical typewriter: Christopher Sholes, Carlos Glidden and Samuel W. Soule, with assistance from James Densmore
- 1868: Air brake (rail): George Westinghouse
- 1869: Motorcycle: Sylvester Roper

THE 1870S
- 1870: Chewing gum: Thomas Adams
- 1870: Magic Lantern projector: Henry R. Heyl
- 1870: Stock ticker: Thomas Alva Edison
- 1871: Cable car (railway): Andrew S. Hallidie
- 1871: Compressed air rock drill: Simon Ingersoll
- 1872: Celluloid (later development): John W. Hyatt
- 1872: Adding machine: Edmund D. Barbour
- 1873: Railway knuckle coupler: Eli H. Janney
- 1873: Blue jeans: Jacob Davis and Levi Strauss
- 1873: Modern direct current electric motor: Zénobe Gramme
- 1874: Electric street car: Stephen Dudle Field
- 1875: Dynamo: William A. Anthony
- 1875: Magazine (firearm): Benjamin B. Hotchkiss
- 1876: Carpet sweeper: Melville Bissell
- 1876: Gasoline carburettor: Daimler
- 1876: Loudspeaker: Alexander Graham Bell
- 1877: Stapler: Henry R. Heyl
- 1877: Induction motor: Nikola Tesla
- 1877: Phonograph: Thomas Alva Edison

- 1877: Toilet paper (rolled): Zeth Wheeler
- 1877: Electric welding: Elihu Thomson
- 1877: Twine knotter: John Appleby
- 1877: Microphone: Emile Berliner
- 1878: Cathode ray tube: William Crookes
- 1878: Transparent film: Eastman Goodwin
- 1878: Rebreather: Henry Fleuss
- 1879: Pelton turbine: Lester Pelton
- 1879: Automobile engine: Karl Benz
- 1879: Cash register: James Ritty
- 1879: Automobile (patent): George B. Seldon
- 1879: Ivory soap: Harley Procter

THE 1880s

- 1880: Photophone: Alexander Graham Bell
- 1880: Roll film: George Eastman
- 1880: Safety razor: Kampfe Brothers
- 1880: Seismograph: John Milne
- 1881: Electric welding machine: Elihu Thomson
- 1881: Metal detector: Alexander Graham Bell
- 1882: Electric fan: Schuyler Skatts Wheeler
- 1882: Electric flat iron: Henry W. Seely
- 1883: Auto engine-compression ignition: Gottlieb Daimler
- 1883: Two-phase (alternating current) induction motor: Nikola Tesla
- 1884: Linotype machine: Ottmar Mergenthaler
- 1884: Fountain pen: Lewis Waterman
- 1884: Punched-card accounting: Herman Hollerith
- 1884: Trolley car (electric): Frank Sprague, Charles Van Depoele

- 1885: Automobile patent granted (internal combustion engine powered): Karl Benz (first automobile put into production)
- 1885: Automobile, differential gear: Karl Benz
- 1885: Maxim gun: Hiram Stevens Maxim
- 1885: Alternating current transformer: William Stanley
- 1886: Dishwasher: Josephine Cochrane
- 1886: Coca-Cola: Dr. John S. Pemberton
- 1886: Gasoline engine: Gottlieb Daimler
- 1886: Improved phonograph cylinder: Tainter & Bell
- 1887: Monotype machine: Tolbert Lanston
- 1887: Contact lens: Adolf E. Fick, Eugène Kalt, and August Muller
- 1887: Gramophone record: Emile Berliner
- 1888: Polyphase AC electric power system: Nikola Tesla (30 related patents)
- 1888: Kodak hand camera: George Eastman
- 1888: Ballpoint pen: John Loud
- 1888: Pneumatic tube tire: John Boyd Dunlop
- 1888: Automobile mobile gasoline engine: Siegfried Marcus
- 1889: Automobile (steam): Sylvester Roper
- 1889: Automobile (gasoline): Gottlieb Daimler
- 1889: Matches (book): Joshua Pusey

THE 1890S
- 1890: Swiss army knife: Carl Elsene
- 1890: Pneumatic hammer: Charles B. King
- 1891: Automobile storage battery: William Morrison
- 1891: Zipper: Whitcomb L. Judson
- 1892: Color photography: Frederic E. Ives
- 1893: Carburetor: Donát Bánki and János Csonka
- 1893: Half-tone engraving: Frederick Ives

- 1893: Wireless communication: Nikola Tesla
- 1893: Radio: Nikola Tesla
- 1893: Kellogg's Corn Flakes: Will Keith Kellogg
- 1894: Radio transmission: Jagdish Chandra Bose
- 1895: Diesel engine: Rudolf Diesel
- 1895: Radio signals: Guglielmo Marconi
- 1895: Shredded Wheat: Henry Perky
- 1896: Vitascope: Thomas Armat
- 1896: Steam turbine: Charles Curtis
- 1896: Electric stove: William S. Hadaway
- 1897: Automobile, magneto: Robert Bosch
- 1897: Modern escalator: Jesse W. Reno
- 1898: Remote control: Nikola Tesla
- 1899: Automobile self-starter: Clyde J. Coleman
- 1899: Magnetic tape recorder: Valdemar Poulsen
- 1899: Gas turbine: Charles Curtis

twentieth century

THE 1900S

- 1900: Rigid dirigible airship: Ferdinand Graf von Zeppelin
- 1900: Hershey bar: Milton Hershey
- 1900: Microwave optics: Jagdish Chandra Bose
- 1901: Improved wireless transmitter: Reginald Fessenden
- 1901: Instant coffee: Sartori Kato
- 1901: Mercury vapor lamp: Peter C. Hewitt
- 1901: Disposable razor blade: King C. Gillette
- 1902: Ostwald process: Wilhelm Ostwald
- 1902: Radio magnetic detector: Guglielmo Marconi
- 1902: Neon lamp: Georges Claude

- 1903: Electrocardiograph (EKG): Willem Einthoven
- 1903: Powered monoplane: Richard Pearse
- 1903: Powered airplane: Wilbur and Orville Wright
- 1903: Bottle machine: Michael Owens
- 1903: Windshield wiper: Mary Anderson
- 1904: Thermionic valve: John Ambrose Fleming
- 1904: Separable attachment plug: Harvey Hubbell
- 1904: Tractor: Benjamin Holt
- 1905: Radio tube diode: John Ambrose Fleming
- 1905: Popsicle: Frank Epperson
- 1906: Sonar (first device): Lewis Nixon
- 1906: Triode amplifier: Lee DeForest
- 1907: Color photography: Auguste and Louis Lumiere
- 1907: Helicopter: Paul Cornu
- 1907: Radio amplifier: Lee DeForest
- 1907: Radio tube triode: Lee DeForest
- 1907: Vacuum cleaner (electric): James Spangler
- 1907: Washing machine (electric): Alva Fisher (Hurley Corporation)
- 1908: Cellophane: Jacques E. Brandenberger
- 1908: Geiger counter: Hans Geiger and Ernest Rutherford
- 1908: Gyrocompass: Hermann Anschütz-Kaempfe
- 1908: Haber process: Fritz Haber
- 1909: Monoplane: Henry W. Walden
- 1909: Gun silencer: Hiram Percy Maxim

THE 1910S
- 1910: Thermojet engine: Henri Coanda
- 1911: Gyrocompass: Elmer A. Sperry
- 1911: Air conditioner: Willis Haviland Carrier

- 1911: Cellophane: Jacques Brandenburger
- 1911: Hydroplane: Glenn Curtiss
- 1913: Crossword: Arthur Wynne
- 1913: Double acting wrench: Robert Owen
- 1913: Gyroscope stabilizer: Elmer A. Sperry
- 1913: Radio receiver, cascade tuning: Ernst Alexanderson
- 1913: Radio receiver, heterodyne: Reginald Fessenden
- 1913: Stainless steel: Harry Brearley
- 1913: X-Ray (improved): William D. Coolidge
- 1914: Liquid fuel rocket: Robert Goddard
- 1914: Tank, military: Ernest Dunlop Swinton
- 1915: Tungsten filament: Irving Langmuir
- 1915: Searchlight arc: Elmer A. Sperry
- 1915: Radio tube oscillator: Lee DeForest
- 1915: Pyrex: Corning Inc.
- 1916: Browning gun: John Browning
- 1916: Thompson submachine gun: John T. Thompson
- 1916: Incandescent gas lamp: Irving Langmuir
- 1917: Cruise missile: Charles Kettering
- 1918: Radio crystal oscillator: A.M. Nicolson
- 1918: Pop-up toaster: Charles Strite
- 1919: Flip-flop circuit: William Eccles and F. W. Jordan

THE 1920S
- 1920: Band-Aid: Earle Dickson
- 1920: Hair dryer
- 1920: Traffic light: William Potts
- 1921: Polygraph: John A. Larson

- 1922: Radar: Robert Watson-Watt, A. H. Taylor, L. C. Young, Gregory Breit, and Merle Antony Tuve
- 1922: Technicolor: Herbert T. Kalmus
- 1922: Water skiing: Ralph Samuelson
- 1923: Arc tube: Ernst Alexanderson
- 1923: Sound film: Lee DeForest
- 1923: Television, electronic: Philo Farnsworth
- 1923: Wind tunnel: Max Munk
- 1923: Xenon flash lamp: Harold Edgerton
- 1925: Ultra-centrifuge: Theodor Svedberg (used to determine molecular weights)
- 1924: Frozen food
- 1925: Television Nipkow System: C. Francis Jenkins
- 1925: Telephoto: C. Francis Jenkins
- 1926: Television mechanical scanner: John Logie Baird
- 1926: Aerosol spray: Rotheim
- 1927: Mechanical cotton picker: John Rust
- 1927: PEZ Candy: Eduard Haas III
- 1927: Photography: First microscopic motion picture camera: Arthur C. Pillsbury
- 1928: Sliced bread: Otto Frederick Rohwedder
- 1928: Electric dry shaver: Jacob Schick
- 1928: Antibiotics: Alexander Fleming
- 1928: Yo-yo: Donald Duncan
- 1929: Electroencephelograph (EEG): Hans Berger

THE 1930S

- 1930: Toll House cookies: Ruth Wakefield
- 1930: Neoprene: Wallace Carothers

- 1930: Nylon: Wallace Carothers
- 1930: Underwater motion picture camera: Arthur C. Pillsbury
- 1931: Radio telescope: Karl Jansky and Grote Reber
- 1931: Iconoscope: Vladimir Zworykin
- 1932: Polaroid glass: Edwin H. Land
- 1935: Microwave radar: Robert Watson-Watt
- 1935: Trampoline: George Nissen and Larry Griswold
- 1935: Monopoly game: Charles Darrow
- 1935: Hammond organ: Laurens Hammond
- 1936: Pinsetter (bowling): Gottfried Schmidt
- 1937: Turboprop engine: György Jendrassik
- 1937: Jet engine: Frank Whittle and Hans von Ohain
- 1937: O-ring: Niels Christensen
- 1938: Ballpoint pen: Laszlo Biro
- 1938: Fiberglass: Russell Games Slayter and John H. Thomas
- 1939: FM radio: Edwin H. Armstrong
- 1939: View-master: William Gruber
- 1939: Automated teller machine: Luther George Simjian

THE 1940S

- 1942: Bazooka rocket gun: Leslie A. Skinner and C. N. Hickman
- 1942: Undersea oil pipeline: Hartley, Anglo-Iranian, Siemens in Operation Pluto
- 1943: Aqua-Lung: Jacques-Yves Cousteau and Emile Gagnan
- 1944: Electron spectrometer: Deutsch Elliot Evans
- 1945: Slinky: Richard James and Betty James
- 1946: Microwave oven: Percy Spencer
- 1946: Bikini swimsuit: Louis Reard
- 1946: Mobile Telephone Service: AT&T and Southwestern Bell

- 1946: Computer: John Mauchly and J. Presper Eckert
- 1947: Transistor: William Shockley, Walter Brattain, and John Bardeen
- 1947: Polaroid camera: Edwin Land
- 1948: Long-playing record: Peter Carl Goldmark
- 1948: Holography: Dennis Gabor
- 1948: Scrabble game: Alfred Butts
- 1949: Atomic clocks

THE 1950S
- 1950: "Peanuts": Charles Schulz
- 1951: Liquid Paper: Bette Nesmith Graham
- 1951: Nuclear power reactor: Walter Zinn
- 1952: Fusion bomb: Edward Teller and Stanislaw Ulam
- 1952: Hovercraft: Christopher Cockerell
- 1954: Geodesic dome: Buckminster Fuller
- 1955: Velcro: George de Mestral
- 1955: Hair spray: Helene Curtis
- 1955: Hard drive: Reynold Johnson with IBM
- 1956: Digital clock
- 1956: Optical fiber: Basil Hirschowitz, C. Wilbur Peters, and Lawrence E. Curtiss
- 1956: Videocassette recorder: Ampex
- 1957: Jet boat: William Hamilton
- 1957: Bubble wrap: Alfred Fielding and Marc Chavannes
- 1958: Integrated circuit: Jack Kilby of Texas Instruments, Robert Noyce at Fairchild Semiconductor
- 1958: Communications satellite: Kenneth Masterman-Smith
- 1959: Snowmobile: Joseph-Armand Bombardier
- 1959: Barbie doll: Ruth Handler

THE 1960S

- 1960: Etch A Sketch: Arthur Granjean
- 1960: Laser: Theodore Harold Maiman
- 1961: Optical disc: David Paul Gregg
- 1963: Computer mouse: Douglas Engelbart
- 1963: Lava Lamp: Edward Craven Walker
- 1965: SuperBall: Norman Stringley
- 1967: Hypertext: Andries van Dam and Ted Nelson
- 1968: Video game console: Ralph H. Baer

THE 1970S

- 1971: E-mail: Ray Tomlinson
- 1971: Liquid Crystal Display: James Fergason
- 1971: Microprocessor
- 1971: Pocket calculator: Sharp Corporation
- 1971: Magnetic resonance imaging: Raymond V. Damadian
- 1971: Floppy disk: David Noble with IBM
- 1971: Karaoke machine: Daisuke Inoue
- 1972: Pong video game: Nolan Bushnell
- 1973: Ethernet: Bob Metcalfe and David Boggs
- 1973: Genetically modified organism: Stanley Norman Cohen and Herbert Boyer
- 1973: Personal computer: Xerox PARC
- 1974: Rubik's Cube: Erno Rubik
- 1974: Hybrid vehicle: Victor Wouk
- 1975: Digital camera: Steven Sasson
- 1976: Gore-Tex fabric: W. L. Gore
- 1977: Personal stereo: Andreas Pavel
- 1977: Cellular mobile phone: Bell Labs

- 1978: Spring-loaded camming device: Ray Jardine
- 1978 : Spreadsheet: Dan Bricklin
- 1979: Trivial Pursuit: Chris Haney and Scott Abbott

THE 1980S

- 1981: Scanning tunneling microscope: Gerd Karl Binnig and Heinrich Rohrer
- 1981: Veggie patty: Paul Wenner
- 1983: Camcorder: Sony
- 1985: DNA fingerprinting: Alec Jeffreys
- 1986: Breadmaker

THE 1990S

- 1990: World Wide Web: Tim Berners-Lee
- 1993: Global Positioning System: United States Department of Defense
- 1993: Beanie Babies: H Ty Warner
- 1997: Non-mechanical digital audio player: SaeHan Information Systems
- 1997: DVD
- 1997: Wi-Fi: Alex Hills
- 1998: Viagra: Nicholas Terret, Peter Dunn, and Albert Wood
- 1998: Google: Sergey Brin and Larry Page

third millennium

2007–2012: Conscious co-creation with Mother Earth?

Glossary

ABUELA: Spanish for Grandmother

ABUELO: Spanish for Grandfather

ABUELO FUEGO: Spanish for Grandfather Fire

COPAL: dried tree resin that is burned during ceremonies in a similar way to incense

KAHULLUMARI: Wirrarika name for the Blue deer spirit who is the guide, messenger, and guardian of the sacred desert of Wirikuta; from the footprints of Kahullumari grow the hikuri (peyote) cactus; the Blue deer emanates the light of the first shaman Grandfather Fire

KAKAIYERI: Wirrarika name for deities and spirits of nature

NAKAWÉ: Wirrarika name for Grandmother Growth

TAYAU: Wirrarika name for Father Sun

ULU TEMAI: Wirrarika name given to me by the eldest shaman of the Wirrarika ceremonial center of Cuexcomatitlan; translations of the name include "New Arrow of the Sun" or "New Ray of the Sun"

WIRRARIKA: Huichol Indian name for the Huichol people that still live in the core ceremonial centers of the Huichol sierra and that carry on the ancient traditions and lifestyles

BIBLIOGRAPHY

Bauval, Robert, and Adrian Gilbert. *The Orion Mystery.* New York, NY: Three Rivers Press, 1994.

Bolen, Jean Shinoda, M.D. *Urgent Message from Mother.* York Beach, ME: Conari Press, 2005.

Calleman, Carl Johan. *The Mayan Calendar and the Transformation of Consciousness.* Rochester, VT: Bear and Company, 2004.

Cohen, Michael J., Ed.D. *Reconnecting with Nature.* Corvallis, OR: Ecopress Books, 1997.

Endredy, James. *Ecoshamanism.* Woodbury, MN: Llewellyn Worldwide, 2005.

The Fatal Harvest Reader. Sausalito, CA: The Foundation for Deep Ecology, 2002.

Fisher, Andy. *Radical Ecopsychology.* Albany, NY: State University of New York, 2002.

Freidel, David, and Linda Schele. *The Untold Story of the Ancient Maya.* New York, NY: William Morrow and Company, 1990.

Freidel, David, Linda Schele, and Joy Parker. *Maya Cosmos*. New York, NY: William Morrow and Company, 1993.

Gore, Al. *An Inconvenient Truth*. New York, NY: Rodale, 2006.

Hutton, William. *Coming Earth Changes*. Virginia Beach, VA: A.R.E. Press, 1996.

Jenkins, John Major. *Galactic Alignment*. Rochester, VT: Inner Traditions, 2002.

———. *Maya Cosmegenesis 2012*. Rochester, VT: Bear & Company, 1998.

László, Ervin. *Science and the Akashic Field*. Rochester, VT: Inner Traditions, 2004.

———. *The Chaos Point*. Charlottsville, VA: Hampton Roads Publishing Co., 2006.

McGuire, Bill. *A Guide to the End of the World*. New York: Oxford University Press, 2002.

Perera, Victor, and Robert D. Bruce. *The Last Lords of Palenque*. Berkeley and Los Angeles, CA: University of California Press, 1982.

Russell, Peter. *Waking Up In Time*. Novato, CA: Origin Press, 1992.

Talbot, Michael. *Mysticism and the New Physics*. Great Britain: Unwin Brothers Limited, 1980.

Tedlock, Barbara. *Time and the Highland Maya*. Albuquerque, NM: University of New Mexico Press, 1992.

White, John. *Pole Shift: Predictions and Prophecies of the Ultimate Disaster.* DoubleDay, 1980.

Zingg, Robert M. *Huichol Mythology*. Tucson, AZ: University of Arizona Press, 2004.

Index

index

index
||||||||||||||||

FREE CATALOG

Get the latest information on our body, mind, and spirit products! To receive a **free** copy of Llewellyn's consumer catalog, *New Worlds of Mind & Spirit,* simply call 1-877-NEW-WRLD or visit our website at www.llewellyn.com and click on *New Worlds.*

LLEWELLYN ORDERING INFORMATION

Order Online:
Visit our website at www.llewellyn.com, select your books, and order them on our secure server.

Order by Phone:
- Call toll-free within the U.S. at 1-877-NEW-WRLD (1-877-639-9753). Call toll-free within Canada at 1-866-NEW-WRLD (1-866-639-9753)
- We accept VISA, MasterCard, and American Express

Order by Mail:
Send the full price of your order (MN residents add 6.5% sales tax) in U.S. funds, plus postage & handling to:

Llewellyn Worldwide
2143 Wooddale Drive, Dept. 978-0-7387-1158-4
Woodbury, MN 55125-2989

Postage & Handling:
Standard (U.S., Mexico, & Canada). If your order is:
$24.99 and under, add $3.00
$25.00 and over, FREE STANDARD SHIPPING

AK, HI, PR: $15.00 for one book plus $1.00 for each additional book.

International Orders (airmail only):
$16.00 for one book plus $3.00 for each additional book

Orders are processed within 2 business days.
Please allow for normal shipping time.
Postage and handling rates subject to change.

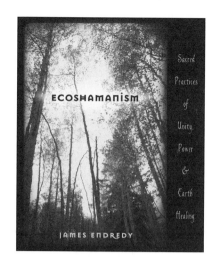

Ecoshamanism

Sacred Practices of Unity, Power & Earth Healing

James Endredy

In a society riddled with rampant consumerism and unsustainable technology, it's easy for everyone, including shamans, to lose touch with the natural world. James Endredy, who has learned from tribal shamans around the globe, presents a new philosophy of shamanic practice called ecological shamanism, or ecoshamanism. Designed to deliver well-being and spiritual harmony, ecoshamanism is the culmination of the visionary practices, rituals, and ceremonies that honor and support nature.

Exploring the holistic perspective of shamanism, Endredy encourages readers to establish a rewarding connection with sacred, life-giving forces using shamanic tools and practices. The author describes more than fifty authentic ecoshamanistic practices—including ceremonies, rituals, chanting, hunting, pilgrimage, and making instruments—that reinforce one's relationship with the natural world.

978-0-7387-0742-6, 7½ x 9⅛, 360 PP. $19.95

To order, call 1-877-NEW-WRLD
Prices subject to change without notice

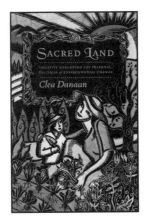

Sacred Land

Intuitive Gardening for Personal, Political, and Environmental Change

Clea Danaan

Clea Danaan breaks new ground with *Sacred Land*—a fresh approach to sacred gardening that goes beyond the backyard.

Danaan shows how the garden can germinate environmental awareness and political change while feeding the spirit. You'll learn how to create compost, save seeds, connect with garden goddesses, perform rituals and magic, and incorporate planetary energy in the garden. Each of the four sections—spanning earth, air, fire, and water—suggest ways of spreading this message of ecology and sustainability to the community. There are also inspiring stories of activists, farmers, artists, healers and other women who are making a difference in the world.

978-0-7387-1146-1, 5 ³⁄₁₆ x 8, 336 pp. $15.95

To order, call 1-877-NEW-WRLD
Prices subject to change without notice

To Write to the Author

If you wish to contact the author or would like more information about this book, please write to the author in care of Llewellyn Worldwide and we will forward your request. Both the author and the publisher appreciate hearing from you and learning of your enjoyment of this book and how it has helped you. Llewellyn Worldwide cannot guarantee that every letter written to the author can be answered, but all will be forwarded. Please write to:

James Endredy
℅ Llewellyn Worldwide
2143 Wooddale Drive, Dept. 978-0-7387-1158-4
Woodbury, MN 55125-2989
Please enclose a self-addressed stamped envelope for reply,
or $1.00 to cover costs. If outside U.S.A., enclose
international postal reply coupon.

Many of Llewellyn's authors have websites with additional information and resources. For more information, please visit our website:

HTTP://WWW.LLEWELLYN.COM